The Smarter STARTUP Real Estate Agent

The Efficient Way to Become a Top 1% Agent FAST

Michael D Regan

WexfordHouseBooks

Copyright © 2024 by Michael D Regan.

All rights reserved.

Printed in the United States of America.

No part of this publication may be reproduced, distributed, or transmitted in any form or by any means, including photocopying, recording, or other electronic or mechanical methods, without the prior written permission of the publisher, except as permitted by U.S. copyright law. For permission requests, contact Wexford House Books.

Cover by Jessica Wright

Editing and Manuscript Design by Shelby Kristoff

First Edition: December 2024

First, thank you to my LORD and Savior Jesus Christ to whom I owe everything.

This book is also dedicated to all the Sales Agents, Client Service Managers, Listing Success Team members, staff, and leaders at Relevate Real Estate whom I've had the honor and pleasure to work with for the past 20 years. Together we created the best real estate brokerage system the world has ever known, and I thank you so much for your ideas, your enthusiasm, your hard work, your willingness to "follow the process", and your patience when our ideas didn't work and we had to fix them (which happened a lot). You all have been one of the biggest and best parts of my life, and there is a lot more fun yet to have together.

And of course... THANK YOU to the over 5,000 buyer and seller clients who have trusted Relevate Real Estate over the years. We have thoroughly enjoyed continually improving our processes to help you sell your homes faster and for high prices, and to help you get the best deal possible on your dream homes and investment properties.

Michael D Regan

Raleigh, NC

December 2024

Contents

CHAPTER 1   2

New Agents Have Three Possible Paths… Choose Wisely, Grasshopper

CHAPTER 2   32

The Ten Different Types of Real Estate Brokerages

CHAPTER 3   46

How To Choose the Best Brokerage for You

CHAPTER 4   66

How To Get Ahead of 99% of Real Estate Agents

CHAPTER 5   80

How To Get Your First Clients in Real Estate

CHAPTER 6   100

The Five BEST Ways to Get Clients in Real Estate

CHAPTER 7   114

The Five WORST Ways to Get Clients in Real Estate

| CHAPTER 8 | 128 |

Three TERRIBLE Career-Crushing Mistakes Real Estate Agents Make When Growing Their Business

| CHAPTER 9 | 142 |

Three HORRIBLE Business-Destroying Mistakes Agents Make When Growing Their Business

| CHAPTER 10 | 156 |

The Truth About Personal Branding: Does It Help Or Hurt?

| Bonus chapters from | 179 |

The Smarter Top Producing Real Estate Agent: Maximize Take-Home Income AND Have Amazing Life Balance

| CHAPTER 1 | 180 |

A Better Way to Be a Top Producing Agent

| CHAPTER 2 | 202 |

The TRUTH About Building Your Own Real Estate Team

Bonus chapters from 219

The Smarter Way to Buy and Sell Your Home: Inside Information from the Mad Scientist of Residential Real Estate

CHAPTER 1 220

The 16 Things Your Agent Must Do When Selling Your Home Part 1

CHAPTER 2 234

How to Find the BEST Home for the BEST Price

PLEASE HELP US IMPROVE

Relevate is a process improvement company that happens to do real estate. This book is one of our products and although we think it's very good, we know it is not perfect. **If you notice anything that does not seem right** (grammar, spelling, formatting), or that is written in a confusing way, or if you have questions we did not answer, or really anything you think could be improved, we would love to hear from you, and listen, and respond. **Please email mike@relevate.life with your feedback.**

CHAPTER 1

New Agents Have Three Possible Paths… Choose Wisely, Grasshopper

Scan QR code for video

If you are a newly licensed agent, or if you have been in the business previously and are looking to restart your career, the alternatives to getting started (or re-started) boil down to three choices. Two of these choices have been around forever, but one of them is new and different... maybe in a good way! In a few pages, I'm going to explore all the details, as well as the advantages and disadvantages, of each of these three choices. But first, let's address an important category of people: those who get a real estate license but don't want to sell.

What If You Want to Do Real Estate, But You DO NOT WANT TO SELL?

Ninety percent of this chapter assumes you like selling and you want to build your real estate sales business to maximize your take-home income. However, many people who get their license very understandably do not want to sell, and since that might be you, I'm going to take a moment to give you two ways to do real estate without selling.

- **Alternative A** is to be a **Licensed Assistant or Transaction Coordinator** working for a busy agent or a team. This role is normally noncommissioned, you get paid for every hour you work, and it sometimes includes bonuses. People who are good at these roles are in high demand! At Relevate Real Estate we have an expanded version of this role called Client Service Manager. We are always hiring great people for this role and if you are interested you can learn more by heading to this article.

- **Alternative B** is to be a **New Construction Onsite Agent.** This role is more customer service than sales because the buyers come to you. Normally this role is paid based on commission. If the neighborhood is hot, you can do great but if the market is slow or your neighborhood is out of the way, the earning potential might not be great. Also, many builders usually require at least two years of real estate experience for on-site agents, so these jobs may be less available to brand new licensees.

Okay, so those were two alternatives for real estate agents who are **not excited about sales.**

How Do I Maximize My Income as a Real Estate Agent?

We are going to shift gears now to the heart of this chapter — agents who want to build their businesses and grow their take-home income as much as possible. For these agents, there are three choices to get started. I will briefly introduce each of these three choices; then, we'll evaluate each according to six important business criteria.

Choice #1 – Buyer's Agent

This involves working on a top agent's team or with a brokerage that provides you with leads (names and contact information of people who are thinking of buying a home). The main advantage of this arrangement is that you immediately have potential clients to talk to. The disadvantage is that oftentimes these leads are not great so you will spend much of your time chasing or serving clients that never close, and you will not keep a lot of the commission. Furthermore, the clients usually belong to the team leader or the firm, so you can't leave the company and keep these clients as the foundation of your own business.

Choice #2 – Individual Agent at a Traditional Brokerage

There are three types of traditional brokerages:

1. There are **big national brand name firms** like Century 21, and Berkshire Hathaway and regional firms like Long & Foster or Howard Hannah. You will pay a large percentage of your commission to work for these large companies.

2. Most of these brand name firms are shrinking now and their agents are moving to low-cost, **mostly virtual national brokerages** like eXp, Fathom, and Real.

3. Finally, there are **smaller local versions of each of those**, often referred to as "boutique brokerages". They are structured the same way as the bigger firms.

The main advantage of all these traditional brokerages is agents are treated in a very "hands-off" way. You will have complete flexibility to do business any way you want to. The main disadvantage is that you must figure out how to grow and manage your business on your own; there is not much training or support beyond the basics of how to fill out the standard contract forms and stay out of legal trouble while serving clients.

Choice #3 – Business System Brokerage

A Business System Brokerage is a proven way to grow and run your real estate business, including continuing marketing and client service support. This approach is not offered by any of the traditional brokerages. The only firm I know of that offers this is our firm, Relevate Real Estate.

As we dig into the details of these three choices, I promise to be as unbiased and objective as possible because my only goal is to help you find the right fit for you. Especially when it comes to the Relevate approach, I will be sure to give you all the disadvantages as well as the advantages.

Evaluating The Three Choices According to Six Business Factors

So, let's dig into each of these three choices for agents who want to build their own businesses, in detail, based on six key factors:

1. Training for how to do real estate

2. Training for how to get clients

3. The cultural and team environment

4. Continuing marketing support

5. Continuing client service support

6. How fast and how big you can expect to grow your business and your take-home income

1. Training For How to Do Real Estate (How to Serve Your Clients)

Wherever you go, the first step is getting trained in how to actually do real estate, in other words, how to legally help all those clients you will be working with.

As a buyer's agent, you will normally get really great training for how to help buyers because the leads you will be given are potential buyers. In most teams, all seller leads belong to the team leader. Although the training for working with buyers will be really good.

At the brand name traditional brokerages, the real estate training will be mostly about how to fill out the agency and offer forms, and how to not get the brokerage in legal trouble. When it comes to the rest of client service, you will need to learn on your own or pay a mentor to help you. When you run into issues during a transaction hopefully, the broker-in-charge will help you, but be prepared to wait in line because there are usually over 100 agents per BIC in larger firms.

The low-cost traditional brokerages like eXp and Fathom are not designed to support or train newer agents. They are really better for agents who already have experience and want the lowest-cost place to hang their licenses.

The traditional "boutique brokerages" are usually very similar to the franchise and low-cost brokerages, but sometimes you can find a brokerage owned by a really great agent who will take you under their wing and teach you everything about real estate. That is amazing if you can find it, and is definitely the best real estate transaction training among the traditional brokerages.

At Relevate, the training for how to do real estate is good and thorough for both buyer and seller transactions. However, there is a reason Relevate can afford to invest so much more in newer agents, and that is because we only accept the highest-potential new agents and there are annual production standards: $2M the first year, $5M the second, and $10M+ after that. So, when agents produce like that, Relevate gets paid back for providing more in-depth training.

2. Training for How to Get Clients (aka "Lead Generation")

Next, you need training for how to actually get clients so you have clients to work with. Being able to get and convert buyer and seller leads is what makes, or breaks, every real estate agent. Every agent can learn the basics of how to fill out paperwork and serve clients … but if you can't get clients to agree to use your services, you will not have any money. That is not good for your future in real estate. Because this topic is so important, we will dig into these details a little deeper.

If you decide to go the buyer's agent route, you will get buyer leads; the names and contact information of real people who allegedly want to buy a home. That is great and is half the battle, but, you will need to know how to convert those leads into clients. The team leaders or brokerages who give you those leads invested a lot of money to get them for you. They either bought them from lead sellers like Zillow or Realtor.com or advertised for them on the radio or social media.

As a result, as a buyer's agent, you will get great training for how to convert buyer leads into clients. The first part of that is to call the lead immediately because often they will go with whoever calls them first. Then, you try to get the buyer to schedule a showing with you, so you can meet them in person and bond with them. The other key part of lead conversion is to stay in touch with all the lukewarm buyers who are not ready yet... because one day they will be.

If you can convert one in 30 purchased leads into a closing, that is really good. According to industry records, last year there were 50 million leads sold to agents, but there were only five million closings, and 75% of those used a referred agent. In other words, 40 leads were sold to agents for every one home that was sold. This means the leads you receive were also given to an average of 40 other agents. So now you see why it is so important to call them quickly.

"At traditional brokerages, you'll have complete flexibility, but you'll have to figure out how to grow and manage your business on your own."

Three Possible Paths for New Agents

Now, sometimes you can find a team leader or brokerage that actually has really high-quality leads. Maybe they have a deal with a corporate relocation company like Graebel. Maybe they have more referred clients than they can handle. Or maybe an agent like my good friend Ellen Pitts has an amazing YouTube channel that brings in buyer leads. In those cases you might close a much higher percentage of leads, like one in five or even one in three. However, in those cases of really good leads, be prepared for the team leader to keep a higher percentage of the commission, like 70%, because what they are giving you is much more valuable than a normal buyer lead.

Traditional franchise brokerages either offer very little training in how to get clients or they offer surface-level training on a smorgasbord of many different approaches. This will include farming, calling FSBOs and expired leads, Search Engine Optimization, pay-per-click advertising, cold calling, direct mail, etc.

There is normally no data presented about which of the many methods is most efficient in terms of money and time in, versus take-home income out.

Whichever lead generation method you choose, be prepared that to be successful you will need to go deep into techniques and dialogues specific to that approach and invest a lot of time and trial and error, to become good enough to actually get enough leads to live on. Do not spread yourself too thin. *Pick one or two methods at the most*, and invest the time and effort to master them, or you will not get the results you need.

One final thought about lead generation at traditional brokerages. The big-name, national companies like Century 21 and RE/MAX talk a lot about brand name recognition, and it is true their names are highly recognizable. However, brand recognition does not equal brand preference. And since, for example, there is no consistency in how various RE/MAX agents deliver their service, there is no defined "RE/MAX" brand experience for consumers to prefer. As a consequence, most experienced agents will tell you that clients choose an agent, not a brand name. The conclusion is, do not count on a brand name to help you get clients.

The Relevate Business System focuses on one type of lead generation: doing business by referral. The advantage is that Relevate's training goes very deep into

"Brand recognition does not equal brand preference. Clients choose an agent, not a brand name. Do not count on a brand name to help you get clients."

every technique needed for success using this lead generation method. Relevate has its own custom CRM software system that organizes you and reminds you what to do next, and once you master this approach you can expect to close two out of every three leads.

The challenge at Relevate is that you need to be comfortable doing business with friends. You have to enjoy getting out and talking to and seeing people in person, and you need to build your own sphere of influence. Relevate will teach you how to do that, but like every other lead generation method, it takes time and work to become successful with it. Also, Relevate does not offer any training or support in any other lead generation methods. That does not mean you can not do them. You just will not get help from Relevate to do so.

3. What is the Cultural and Team Environment?

An important factor for most agents is the cultural environment of a brokerage.

As a buyer's agent, you are on a team. A good team leader will foster healthy and motivating competition. Sometimes, however, it can feel like a little too much competition. For example, if the same lead is sent to multiple team members at the same time, and everyone is glued to their phones to make sure they claim it first. In addition, some team leaders give more and better leads to the agents who have the best history of converting those leads into commission checks. That is an understandable policy, but it can create hard feelings among the team.

In a traditional brokerage, management does their best to foster camaraderie among the agents and a sense of community, and many do a remarkably good job. But, that can be a difficult task for two reasons. First, in a traditional brokerage, each agent uses a different database management system, not connected in any way to other agents' databases. Therefore, there can be a lot of overlap between client bases. As a result, in some cases, two or three agents from the same office end up competing for the same client. This competition makes agents less likely to share ideas and information with each other, and can even result in hard feelings and some unhealthy types of competition.

In the Relevate Business System model, everyone uses the same connected database management system, and any overlaps are flagged the second an agent adds a new person to their sphere of influence, far in advance of any referrals and resulting transactions. Because overlaps are discovered immediately, before any potential commission is involved, they are almost always resolved amicably, like "Hey, you take this person, I will take the next." As a result, the possibility of competition for the same clients is avoided, and agents feel good about sharing ideas and helping each other.

The cultural challenge at Relevate is that many of the most productive agents are just not around the office very much. The Relevate marketing and client service support free them up to do other things besides work all the time, and they are out doing those other things. For the sake of our newer agents, we wish more top producers were around more often.

4. Ongoing Marketing Support

The next criteria by which we are evaluating different places to start your real estate business is marketing support. This is not about teaching you how to market to prospective clients, this is helping you actually do it consistently and with high quality.

If you start as a buyer's agent, some team leaders will invest in a service to call and confirm the leads to make sure they are real and high quality, before they get to you, which can save you a ton of time. And maybe even more importantly, some team leaders will also help you keep in touch with those "someday maybe" buyers by doing quarterly or even monthly emails or mailings. Be grateful for those team leaders because that will definitely help you sell more homes.

As an individual agent at a traditional brokerage, in general, it is up to you to think of, plan, and execute your marketing ideas. Some managers may offer you some free hours of help from the office assistant, which is great. Unfortunately, most agents are either too busy with client work to focus on marketing or do not have enough money coming in to afford marketing, so it just does not happen consistently and the business suffers.

In the Relevate Business System model, the marketing department plans marketing campaigns each year in advance for each upcoming year. They are designed, printed, and ready to go for the agents, who can then choose to participate or not. The cost is low because they are done for all agents at the same time. The agents are fine with that because their spheres of influence do not overlap. So agents get consistent marketing for a low price without any work required on their part. That obviously brings them more clients.

The two disadvantages are, first, although monthly campaigns are voluntary participation based, agents do pay for all the campaigns in which they participate. Second, if an agent wants to do their own unique campaign the marketing department can help them with it, but that campaign will cost the agent relatively more than the pre-planned monthly campaigns because the fixed costs will not be shared by all the other agents, because that agent is the only one doing that one unique campaign.

5. Ongoing Client Service Support

The fifth factor in deciding how to start your real estate business is the Client Service Support provided by the firm or brokerage. This factor is important because it allows you to focus more on gaining new clients instead of being too busy delivering the service yourself.

If you decide to start as a buyer's agent, your team leader will probably provide a trained transaction coordinator to handle "contract to close" tasks, to free you up to spend more time converting leads, showing homes, and writing contracts. Depending on how much of the commission the team leader keeps, you may have to pay for this, or the team leader may pay for the transaction coordinators. Either way, this is a win for everyone. The big value in a team is created when leads are converted. That is the hard part that takes the most skill. If you are good at that, it is in everybody's interest, especially yours, to spend as much time on that as possible.

Some traditional brokerages also have trained transaction coordinators on staff ready to help you and again depending on your deal with the brokerage either you or they will pay for it. The advantage is that you can spend more time doing the activity that creates the most value for you and your brokerage, lead generation, and conversion. It is totally worth it if, while the transaction coordinator is doing the contract to close tasks, you are out there getting more clients. This is smart business; you will not grow past a certain point without this kind of help.

However, at a traditional brokerage, when you get even busier, you will need to hire, train, and manage your own transaction coordinators. When you get even busier you will need to become a team leader yourself and hire buyer's agents and invest in providing leads for them, because you will not be able to handle all the client work yourself. This works for some agents but the disadvantage is that an agent who was great at lead generation has now become a manager and a lead buyer. Because of the time and expense and the need to pay buyer's agents 50%+ of the total commission to keep them, you end up working 60+ hours per week and not actually taking home a lot of money.

The Relevate Business System provides an advanced version of a transaction coordinator called a Client Service Manager, or CSM. These are fully licensed agents who are trained to take everything off the plates of busy agents other than lead generation, lead conversion, and contract negotiation. However, the agent does not get to "hand off" the client to the CSM, they both continue to work with the client together, very similar to a doctor and a nurse, each doing their role, as a well-oiled team. As a result, the agent can focus on getting more clients and also have a balanced life. The client feels they got two agents for the price of one, which is never a bad thing.

The challenge of this part of the Relevate model is that, although you can use as much or as little CSM support as you wish, you do have to pay for this help. Also, you have to learn to be a good teammate with the CSM and learn to trust someone other than yourself to help take good care of your clients. Relevate provides plenty of training for agents to achieve this, but that is still a challenge for most agents while they are learning.

6. How Fast and How Big Can I Grow My Income as a New Agent?

Okay, so we have looked at each potential way to start up your real estate business. Let's look at how fast and how big you can grow your business and income in each situation.

Being a buyer's agent is the fastest way to start working with actual buyers and so is also theoretically the fastest way to start earning income, assuming you are good at converting those buyer leads. So that is the advantage. The disadvantages are, first, the clients do not belong to you (in most cases), so you are not building a client base to take with you when you want to go out on your own. Second, you will not learn to work with sellers, and listings are kind of important in real estate. Third, at least two-thirds of those who start as buyer's agents seem to get addicted to the leads being given to them, and to the hustle of chasing them. These agents can not escape because they are not willing to step out as an individual agent and learn how to generate their own leads, for themselves. So they get stuck only earning 50% of the commission, or less, for the rest of their careers. Even worse, since they can only delegate contract-to-close, they work tons of hours.

At a traditional brokerage, you can grow as fast as you get great at one (or maybe two) lead generation and conversion methods. Once you do get going though, you will soon hit a ceiling of how much you can do all by yourself, and that is when you will need to learn to be a manager so you can effectively hire, train, and lead a team of transaction coordinators and buyer's agents. The advantage of this is that you will close a lot of volume and other agents will admire your success. However, as we discussed earlier, the disadvantage is that this team structure requires a lot of working hours from the team leader, and the expenses are very high. Some team leaders even lose money if the revenue from the team does not cover all the costs of generating leads.

If you are investigating working with a traditional brokerage, I suggest asking them this question: "Let's say I want to be a top-producing agent selling $10 million or more annually, but I do not want to 60+ hours a week or become a team manager. Do you have any way to support me or help me so that neither of those things will happen to me when I get to $10 million?"

I would love to hear what they say because I don't think traditional brokerage offers a good answer to that.

When it comes to how fast and how big you can grow in **The Relevate Business System,** the biggest advantage and biggest challenge are actually the same. Relevate only accepts agents who have the ability and determination to grow their businesses to $10M+ in regular annual volume. If you have both the ability and the determination, we have the system that can help you get there from zero within two years. Now, not everyone gets there in two years, so our standards are $2M in the first year, $5M in the second year, and $10M in the third year. Now, again, we do have some that get to the $5M mark and not quite to $10M in the third year, and as long as they are working as hard and as smart as they can, we will continue to support them toward the $10M annual goal.

Okay, so right now, as you think about what I just explained, you are either excited and pumped and want to be in that situation with those growth expectations! Or you are thinking ... can I really do that? Or more likely, do I even want to do that?

Now, if part of your thinking is "Hey Mike, I don't want to have to work tons of hours for the rest of my life just to sell homes and make money. If that is what it takes, I don't want it."

Well, that is why we have the marketing and client service support. To free you up so you can have a great business and a great life. Think about it, most business owners, when their business gets successful, work less, not more. That is how it should be in real estate too. And that's what the Relevate Business System is set up to do. But in the beginning, you do need to be willing to work hard at working smart. We will teach you if you want to learn.

Buyer's Agent, Traditional Brokerage, or Relevate Business System?

As a new agent or an agent looking to restart your real estate business, you can either be a buyer's agent, join a traditional brokerage, or join the Relevate Business System.

Your choice comes down to what you want to accomplish in your real estate business, and how you want to do it. How much money do you want to earn and how important is that to you? How important is work-life balance for you and your family? How important is it to do things your way, as opposed to learning a proven system?

The fastest way to get started and get a paycheck is by being a buyer's agent. But you will not learn how to generate leads or work with sellers, and you will not be building your own business. Making the leap from being a buyer's agent to having your own real estate sales business can be tough, but it is definitely doable for a hardworking, smart person like you.

Joining a big, established brand name traditional brokerage is still **by far the most popular choice**. You will have complete freedom to invent your own business systems for finding and serving clients. That can start out exciting… but can get frustrating if you do not get traction. When you do get traction you can find yourself in a situation where you are working more than you want to, or having to become a manager and build a team.

The **working-by-referral focus, production standards, and teamwork approach** of the Relevate Business System can be exciting if that is exactly what you want. If it is not the right fit for you, it would definitely be best to jump into being a buyer's agent or joining a traditional brokerage.

"I got into real estate because I had already accomplished everything I could as a teacher, and I was ready to achieve bigger goals. I joined Relevate because they are know for turning ambitious new agents into top producers and that's what I wanted to be, as soon as possible.

From the beginning, the existing top producers were totally there to mentor me. They didn't look at me as competition, they wanted to help me, and now that I'm one of them I'm happy to do that for other new agents.

Second, my office had not one but three brokers in charge who were always available to answer all my hundreds of questions.

Third, Relevate has proprietary software that tells you exactly what to do each day to be successful, including a point system and scoreboard that motivates you; because it's proven that if you DO the points, you'll BECOME a top-producing agent.

The process worked great for me.

I closed $9.2 million in my first year, and thirty-one million in my second full year for which I am more than grateful. I didn't tell you yet that **I'm also a mom to three young kiddos.** The client service support team at Relevate enabled me to handle all that business, and that's one of many reasons I will never leave."

Laura Richardson

Scan QR code for video

CHAPTER 2

The Ten Different Types of Real Estate Brokerages

Scan QR code for video

Ten Different Types of Real Estate Brokerages

I've put this list in order from roughly how long each type of brokerage has existed on planet earth, from oldest to newest. I'm not aware of the timeline of brokerages on other planets. The first few have been around on our planet for over 70 years, and the last of the list has only been around for about 15 years. I'm not going to recommend any one over another. It all comes down to what type of brokerage is the best fit for you. With that in mind, after hearing about each type of brokerage, stop for a moment to reflect on what you want from a brokerage, verses what this type of brokerage claims to offer, and ask yourself if that type of firm might be the best fit for you. So, here we go...

1. The first type of brokerages are LOCAL BOUTIQUE FIRMS. The primary benefit they claim to provide agents is that they are "small and local, and you'll have a nice group of quality people to get to know and work with." Other than that, these types of firms do not have any typical characteristics. Every boutique firm is different. Some are very high-end, while others are similar to low-cost firms. They often incorporate elements from the other types of firms listed below. High-quality examples of these types of

firms in the Raleigh-Durham area are The Rich Realty Group, Urban Durham Realty, and Inhabit Real Estate.

2. NATIONAL AND REGIONAL BRAND firms came along next, when a number of local boutique firms expanded to other cities and states. These firms have spent a ton of money on brand recognition, and their main claim is that "Our highly recognized brand name will help you get more clients." These firms typically have excellent brokers-in-charge, solid training for new agents, big offices, medium cost to the agent. High quality examples of these firms include C21, Coldwell Banker, Berkshire Hathaway, Long & Foster, Weichert, Howard Hannah, and many other firms with high regional or local brand recognition. These types of firms would be good for any agent who feels that national brand recognition would be a significant help to their business.

3. The next type of brokerage are those that specialize in NEW CONSTRUCTION SALES. These firms sell agents on the idea that you will

"Work out of a beautiful model home, and customers come to you." This could be a role within a brokerage or working directly with the builder. The compensation can be great and steady in a good neighborhood in a strong market. You will need to be prepared to work almost every weekend, because that's when new customers stop by most often. Local examples of these types of firms are Toll Brothers, Ashton Woods, and the Jim Allen Group.

4. The fourth type of brokerage are the LOW COST firms. These firms compete on being... low cost for agents, not necessarily for buyers and sellers... that's up to each individual agent. Their claim is simply "We charge you very little to hang your license with us." These firms claim to be, and usually are, very inexpensive to work with, but of course they offer limited broker-in-charge, or any other type of support. Fathom Realty and Realty One are two great examples of these types of firms. If you are convinced there is nothing that a brokerage can do to add value for your business, this type of brokerage would be your best choice.

5. Gary Keller made the TEAM AND BRAND BUILDING brokerages famous with the book *The Millionaire Real Estate Agent.* This type of firm specializes in giving agents guidance to build their own team and brand. If you want to hire, train, and manage your own team and have your own logo and brand name, this type of firm is perfect for you. Keller Williams is the biggest of these brokerages, and newcomers Side and Fusion offer even more advanced versions of the same approach. If you are convinced that building and leading a team is the best strategy for your future, this type of brokerage will be perfect for you. You can check out my book, *The Smarter Top Producing Agent* for an unbiased analysis of the different ways to have the support team you will need to grow your business beyond 20 or so transactions per year, and maybe even have a life outside of real estate.

6. The next type of brokerages are LEAD PROVIDERS. These firms advertises for, or purchases cold leads, and teaches mostly new agents how to convert these leads into clients, and then into commission checks. They typically

provide great training, because they must, because it's hard to convert those types of leads, and they generally keep at least half the commission because those leads are expensive. These are very professionally managed organizations such as DASH Carolinas or Paracle locally. If you are a new agent who needs experience, this type of firm may be a good choice. However, you'll keep a low percentage of your commission revenue, and you'll be learning how to handle cold leads, which frankly isn't a whole lot of fun for most agents. Too many agents get addicted to cold leads, and that's a formula for a very exhausting career. The key will be to learn to cultivate relationships with past clients so you'll start getting tons of referral business, which is much better business, and this type of LEADER PROVIDER brokerage may not have the software tools or coaching or support to help you make that change.

7. MULTI-LEVEL marketing has been used to sell all kinds of products and the next type of firm focuses almost exclusively on using multi-level reward systems to recruit agents. They promise

that you will be able to earn unlimited passive income by recruiting other agents, and the agent who recruited you will be financially motivated to help you. The biggest and best example is eXp Realty, but Exit Realty paved the way years before them. If your primary interest is recruiting and not selling homes, these types of firms could be perfect for you.

8. The seventh type of brokerage is YOUR OWN BROKERAGE. There are only three reasons to start your own brokerage. The most common is because you want to develop your own unique brand that means something different in the market. That's tough to do as part of a bigger brokerage because legally you are required to show their name and logo also in your advertising, and that's confusing to consumers. So that's a good reason to start your own firm. The second reason is to save money by not having to pay anything to a firm. Very few agents start their own firm for this reason, because there are so many truly low cost brokerages now, where you can hang your license for next to nothing. The third reason is because you feel you

Ten Different Types of Real Estate Brokerages

have a better way to do real estate, and you want to do it your way. If you do it for this third reason, be prepared that if you want agents to join your firm, you'll need to give them value worth more to them than what they are paying you. Tall order. I don't have any examples for you of firms started by you. You'll have to create your own.

9. Are you a new agent and wish you could help people buy and sell homes and also have a BASE SALARY AND BENEFITS? Well, with this next type of brokerage, you can do that. Redfin is the most well-known brokerage that offers this to agents. This is like the "Lead Provider" model, but they don't have salary and benefits, and Redfin does. If you work hard at this type of firm, you can not only have some security, but you will take home more than the average agent. If you take the risk in a commission-only situation, you can take home much more income, even if your first years. It just comes down to how smart and how hard you are willing to work.

10. The tenth, and most recent type of brokerage are those that FOCUS ON SYSTEMS AND

PROCESS IMPROVEMENT. This type of firm promises that "Our systems will help you work smarter, give better client service, make more money, and better work life balance." The proven processes and support at these types of firms will deliver the promised results IF you use them correctly. The results theoretically more than pay for the cost of the productivity-enhancing structure and support staff. This type of brokerage is best for agents who naturally seek to do everything in life in the smartest and most efficient way, who don't like to waste time re-inventing systems and processes for themselves, and who value structure and consistency as an essential part of running a successful business.

So there you have it, the ten different types of real estate brokerages. Now comes the hard part.... which is best for you? Think through that list again. Which are the two or three, or even one type of brokerage that resonates most with you as an agent? What do you value most in your career as a real estate agent? Which from the list above aligns closest with these values?

Ten Different Types of Real Estate Brokerages

"Take a few minutes to ask yourself the right questions to understand what you want from a brokerage so you can make sure they have what you want when you meet with them."

So, What Type of Real Estate Brokerage Is Right For You?

We gave you just a few examples of brokerages within each category, but we'll be happy to recommend additional high-quality organizations in your city within the type of brokerage in which you are interested. PRO TIP: Most agents, whether they are looking for their first brokerage or leaving their current firm, are in a hurry to interview brokerages and are looking for the right questions to ask them. But you'll help yourself in a big way by taking a few minutes to **ask yourself the right questions to understand what you want from a brokerage** so you can make sure they have what you want when you meet with them.

"I decided to get into real estate as a professional career because I wanted to leverage my time and my energy and my knowledge. I wanted to make executive level income, without going through the bureaucratic mess of the corporate world.

I wanted a brokerage that had really well-thought-out processes and systems that I could leverage and make my own. I wanted to create a business that would give me a predictable income stream, that I could rely on whether the market's up, or whether the market's down.

When I joined Relevate, I found the systems and processes I expected, AND the support I was used to in the corporate world and as a military officer. Everything they explained to me came true. Business started to happen, income started to happen, and eventually within a relatively short amount of time, my business grew exponentially. Agents at other places who started around the same time that I did had very limited success, even in a very good market. And now, even in a down market, I'm having my best year ever.

Part of who I am is I want to share what's good with other people. I want other agents to have the same experience I'm having, to have the exponential growth I've experienced. If any of what I've said resonates with the questions you're asking, I'm happy to have a conversation. Reach out to me, and we'll set up time and I'll explain what my life has looked like here and what you could expect here as well."

Pete Marston

Scan QR code for video

CHAPTER 3

How To Choose the Best Brokerage for You

Scan QR code for video

Choosing the right brokerage can bring big positive changes to your business and your life. But choosing the wrong brokerage can result in disappointment and disruption. I've discovered one important activity almost every agent skips in their process of choosing a brokerage. This activity will not only make all the difference when it comes to choosing the right brokerage for you, but it may also change the entire direction of your career.

As the leader of a mid-sized brokerage, I've interviewed hundreds of agents. Many were a good fit for us and we have had great success here. I've recommended many other agents to other local brokerages I thought would be a better fit for them than us. In any case, over the years, I've learned a lot about how these agents could have made better decisions about which brokerage was the right fit for them.

The problem I've seen so many times is that most agents go into the process of choosing a brokerage without having put any real thought into the goals they have for their real estate business, how they want to run their business, and as a result, what they need from their brokerage. In this chapter, I will explain why this is so important, and I'll give you 10 highly thought-provoking questions to ask yourself, to clarify what is most important for you. Finally, I'll share six quick examples of agents who asked themselves these questions, and which specific brokerages ended up being the right fit for them.

Understand What Types of Systems and Support You Need from a Real Estate Brokerage

Many agents never stop thinking about how they want their business and life as a real estate agent to work. For example, there are ways to do business that involve managing and motivating other people, and other ways that allow you to focus only on what you love to do and are best at. There are ways to do real estate that will grind you up and leave you exhausted and poor, and other ways that will enable you to get ahead and retire with plenty of money in the bank.

Depending on how you want your business and life to work, you'll need very different types of systems and support from your brokerage. Below, **I've listed 10 key questions (plus 17 more BONUS questions) that will help you gain a clear understanding of this for**

"Depending on how you want your business and life to work, you'll need very different types of systems and support from your brokerage."

yourself. Let's dive into these questions and get you one step closer to where you want to be in your career.

For each of the questions below, ask yourself which choice is right for you… then ask yourself why? What are you hoping to achieve (or avoid) by going in that direction?

1. Are you looking to make (a) a full-time take-home income from your real estate business, or (b) would a few commissions each year be all you really need?

2. What parts of the real estate business are you great at and love to do, and which parts are you either not good at or don't like to do (or both)?

3. Do you have a preferred way of acquiring clients? In other words, do you prefer referrals, advertising, social media, farming neighborhoods, or calling FSBO and expireds? Or a mix of many methods? What makes you prefer that way of acquiring clients?

4. Do you want (a) to manage all aspects of your business as you grow, or (b) would you rather

focus on bringing in the business and have support (professionally hired, trained, and managed by someone else) for other parts of your business, as needed?

5. Is building your own team an important goal for you? If so, is that more because (a) you want to lead other people or (b) because you want to maximize your income?

6. How important is it for you to (a) have control of your time, especially your evenings and weekends, and to be able to take a vacation and be fully unplugged and still be sure your clients are being well taken care of? Or (b) do you not need "downtime" and are fine with responding to client needs whenever needed?

7. Are you more interested in (a) developing your own systems and processes for your business, or (b) do you want to plug into pre-existing and proven processes and systems?

8. Regarding marketing, do you (a) consistently develop your own creative marketing campaigns in advance so you always have a reason to call

your sphere of influence, or (b) would you really rather have someone else do a great job of that for you?

9. Which is more important to you, (a) recognition of your sales volume and number of transactions or (b) maximizing take-home income?

10. Is minimizing the amount of money you pay the brokerage (a) the main priority to you, or (b) are you willing to pay the brokerage more if you are getting a good return on your investment from that money?

17 More Bonus Questions…

1. Are you (a) expecting (or hoping) that a brokerage will bring value to help achieve your business goals, or (b) feeling that brokerage for you is mostly a place to fulfill the legal requirement to "hang your license" while you run your independent business?

2. Is it (a) important for you to have a highly skilled, accessible broker-in-charge or (b) is BIC support something you rarely ever need?

3. Do you (a) value having other successful agents around to collaborate with, or (b) already have all the knowledge and motivation you need?

4. Is it (a) important to have your brokerage near your home? If so, how close is close enough? Do you want to have an office? Or (b) is it okay if the office is a bit of a drive, but you still want a physical office in which you can interact in person with other agents, or (c) is a virtual brokerage (no offices, virtual training, and meetings) right for you?

5. Are you (a) interested in mentoring other agents (eventually or now) and having input to continuous improvement at your brokerage, or (b) do you have too much already going on that you would not have time for this type of activity?

6. Regarding finances, do you tend to (a) live paycheck to paycheck (and maybe owe back taxes), or (b) have at least some savings and pay more-than-estimated quarterly tax payments, so

you don't have to worry about tax surprises each April?

7. Do you feel (a) there is a possibility of new and much more effective ways to run your real estate business, or (b) are you satisfied that you already know the best ways to run your business?

8. Do you feel that (a) your brokerage's brand name recognition is very important to your ability to successfully acquire clients, or (b) your brokerage's brand name recognition doesn't make much of a difference?

9. Would it be important that (a) your brokerage enforces minimum production standards to motivate you and ensure you are surrounded by successful agents, or (b) no, that wouldn't matter because either you work independently or you associate with the agents you choose, regardless of what brokerage they are a part of?

10. Are you the type to refer other agents to your brokerage? If so, is it important for you to be (a) rewarded financially based on their

performance, or (b) are you fine with being thanked only with non-financial appreciation?

11. Are you (a) good at tracking and documenting your revenues and expenses for tax purposes, or (b) would it be helpful to have that built into the services provided by your brokerage?

12. Do you feel that (a) the only way to serve a client well (and to build a relationship with them) is to do everything yourself, or (b) it could be possible to maintain your relationship with the client and provide them with good service if you delegated much of the client service to highly-trained professional licensed agents following a well-documented process?

13. Is your business philosophy more (a) "I'm open (and even eager) to spending money on systems and support that give me a good return on investment" or (b) "all costs are expenses, and they should be cut if possible"?

14. When it comes to selling (i.e. acquiring clients), would you (a) rather have methods to find your own clients, (b) pay for leads or referral fees for

clients from someone else, or (c) not sell at all and partner with a "team leader" to help serve their clients? Are you okay with (a) selling your services to friends, or would you (b) rather deal mostly with people you don't know other than their interest in buying or selling?

15. Regarding your earning goals, which statement is "more you": (a) I only need so much, and wanting more is greedy and maybe even wrong, or (b) I want to earn as much as possible because it gives me freedom, and the ability to give money away to good causes?

16. Do you feel that (a) every activity in your business is of equal value, or (b) there are some activities that produce much more value for you than other activities? If so, what are those activities in your business?

17. Do you feel individual branding (meaning other than your personal name and photo, such as a business name and logo specific to you, in addition to the name and logo of your brokerage) is (a) important to you, or (b) not important to

your success (beyond your personal name and photo)?

Identify the Real Estate Brokerages that Provide the Systems and Support You Need

Now that you've done such good thinking, underline or highlight your top three to five answers to the questions above that point to the most important factors for you. Next, do your research to uncover which brokerages specialize in providing the types of systems and support that will help you do business and life the way you want to.

TIP: Some brokerages try to be "all things to all agents", which means they are mediocre at everything, and you don't want to be mediocre, right? The goal of these firms is a high agent count — they will accept almost anyone. They haven't fine-tuned any approach to doing real estate. They don't have core values agents need to conform to, no expectations agents need to meet, or minimum production standards. They just want tons of agents.

You need a brokerage that specializes in what you need. Here is an example.

"DASH Carolinas" in Raleigh, NC is run by a great guy named Quentin Dane. DASH is great in one specific way of doing real estate: purchasing Zillow leads and training their agents to convert them into closings and commission checks. If you are into that, you'll do great at DASH. If you are not into that, they'll suggest a different brokerage that might be a better fit. They've sent agents to us, and we've sent agents to them. DASH knows what types of agents are right for DASH. They don't try to be everything for everyone. That's the kind of brokerage you want.

Once you've identified several brokerages that provide the kinds of systems and support you need, it's time to interview the leaders of that brokerage, and several agents who have been there for several years.

Use These Tips to Learn the Real Priorities of Each Real Estate Brokerage

Now that you know what you want, don't compromise! You need to find out what each brokerage stands for compared to what you want.

HERE'S HOW: As I mentioned earlier, many brokerages simply want high agent count, and during interviews they will try to find out what you want, then tell you they've got the "perfect systems and support" for that. You need to find out what they really think, before you tell them what you want. So, don't tip them off about what you hope to hear from them. Ask them questions to learn who they really are and what they really think.

For example, if you want help building a team, don't ask, "Can you help me build a team?" but instead ask, "What is your philosophy about agents building teams? Do you think it is a good idea for them to do that?" If you want help to get more referred clients, ask, "What do you think is the best way for agents to market themselves to get more clients?" rather than asking, "Do you have training and systems to help me get more referred clients?" Lastly, if you want help planning and executing your marketing, ask, "What are your thoughts about agent marketing? Should each agent plan/write/design/execute that for themselves, or should they delegate that?" Don't ask, "Do you have a marketing team that will help me plan and execute my marketing?"

Notice the questions in the second column give away what you want the brokerage to tell you, whereas the questions in the third column make it necessary for the brokerage to commit to how they really think a real estate business should be run. You want to be with a firm where their leaders think the way you want them to; not a firm that tells you what you want to hear.

The best brokerages will be straightforward about their answers without regard to what they think you want to hear. They only want agents who are a good fit for them. They are focused on being great at one way of doing business, and if what they do great is what you want, that's the place for you.

I hope that after all your good research and interviewing, you will be confident in your next choice of brokerage. Let's look at a few real-life examples of how agents chose the brokerage they joined.

Example of Agents and The Real Estate Brokerages They Chose

We have had several hundred agents come to talk with us, many of them were a perfect fit for us, and others were a fit for a different brokerage. These examples are based on our conversations with real agents (although we have changed their names here to protect their privacy):

- For Makoto, the most important priorities were: (i) learning to build her own team, (ii) freedom and encouragement to build her own brand, (iii) potential for passive income, and (iv) a library of systems and processes to choose from. For Makoto, the ideal choice was Keller Williams Realty.

- The important priorities for Anna were: (i) reasonably high earning opportunity, (ii) having processes and systems to plug into, (iii) not having to find her own clients, and (iv) having an out-of-home office. Being an onsite agent at Fonville Morisey Barefoot New Homes ended up being a great fit for Anna.

- George cared most strongly about (i) being able to work from his home office, (ii) having his own personal brand and logo, (iii) relatively low-cost brokerage, and (iv) he had no need for close BIC support. For George, eXp Realty was the perfect choice.

- As a newer agent, Becky told us she needed (i) great real estate transaction training, (ii) a brokerage with very strong national brand recognition, and (iii) a very good BIC with plenty of time to train her and oversee her transactions. Becky made a great decision to join Berkshire Hathaway (Coldwell Banker would have been another excellent choice).

- Jose's top priorities were: (i) reasonably high-earning opportunities, (ii) not having to find his own clients, (iii) excellent training, and (iv) a high-energy environment to keep him motivated. Jose joined Better Homes and Gardens Paracle (DASH Carolina would have also been a great choice).

- Finally, as a mother of two young children, Katya values: (i) being home weekends and evenings, (ii) high minimum production standards to ensure she's surrounded by successful agents, (iii) having proven processes and systems to plug into, and (iv) a CRM that supports working by referral. For Katya, Relevate Real Estate ended up being the best choice.

Which Real Estate Brokerage is Right for You?

Choosing the right brokerage is a difficult decision. The right systems and support will set you up for big business growth, and hopefully more time to enjoy life with family and friends. The wrong decision will result in disappointment and disruption.

You now have 10 questions that will help you understand exactly what you need from a brokerage for it to be the right fit for you. Once you've got that figured out, you can do the research to identify which firms provide systems and support you need. Our research revealed that all brokerages actually fit into one of 10 different types, each claiming to offer unique advantages for agents.

We already introduced you to DASH Carolinas as one quality choice for agents who want what they do well, but we haven't discussed who is a good fit for us here at Relevate. We focus on systems to do business by referral and helping agents with marketing and client service support. We are not the right brokerage for every agent, but we're the perfect fit for agents that want what we specialize in providing.

"When I first started in real estate, I knew I really wanted to help people, but I quickly realized getting business was actually the most difficult thing in real estate. So when I was listening to what other firms had to offer, it was mostly about their brand name, or throwing me on a team. But there weren't really any processes they were presenting to me on how to help me get clients and grow my OWN business. You had to figure it out on your own basically.

Relevate Real Estate offered an actual system that was PROVEN. It was very human-centric, really relationship driven, which is very much in line with what I wanted in my work. I wanted to be able to connect with people on a deeper level. And then very quickly, it actually worked. In my second year I closed 38 transactions and was over $10 million in volume.

Even more important though, the marketing and client service support teams here allowed me not get lost in my work and still spend time with my wife and four young kids, who are involved in a lot of cool activities. Three times a week I bring them to ju jitsu, then we have dance and theater, and spending every evening together.

I couldn't imagine being too busy to do those things with them. The ability to still serve clients well, and still have time for my family has been really valuable to me.

So I'm really grateful. And I'm not one to find something good and just keep it to myself. I want good for other people. So if you want to meet up, I'd be happy to share my story and answer any questions you have. Just text or call me and we'll get together."

Matt Minor

Scan QR code for video

CHAPTER 4

How To Get Ahead of 99% of Real Estate Agents

Scan QR code for video

R eal Estate is a 90/10 business, meaning 90% of the sales and the money are made by 10% of the agents. But even within that top 10%, the top 1% take home nearly half the income. What makes them different? What do you have to do to be in that 1%?

In my 17-year career I sold over 750 homes and was well within the top 1% of real estate agents nationally. I know what it took to get to that level, and honestly, it didn't take superhuman ability and I didn't have to work myself to the bone for a decade. If you are willing to work hard for a little while, and more importantly work very smart, you can be a top 1% real estate agent within a few short years.

The first thing you need to do to become a top 1% real estate agent, and this is tough but real is …

1. FORGET Having a Balanced Life for Your First Year In Real Estate

Many people get into real estate thinking they'll have freedom and a flexible schedule, but what they don't realize is that the only agents who have that are either

(a) those who aren't doing any business, or

(b) those who worked very hard during their first year in business to build their foundation, so that they are now able to handle a large volume of business and still have a balanced life.

Nothing in life is free, so if you want that result, you'll need to push really hard to get established early on. If you never make that sustained push at the beginning, you won't get anywhere near being a top 1% agent. You need a year of 150% effort, sacrificing other parts of your life temporarily, if you want to get near the top of this profession.

If you didn't invest that year at the beginning of your career, you can start at any time. The sooner you start, the sooner it will be done and over with forever.

Now, at this point, some will say, "Well, I'm not going to sacrifice time with my family to chase the almighty dollar." It's fine with me if you want to feel that way, but if so, I think you're completely missing the point. Your family might see you half as much for a year, but if you build the foundation of your business the right way, they'll see you twice as much for the rest of your life, you'll have financial security, and you'll be able to take some amazing vacations with them.

I know this from experience… being a top real estate agent for ten years paid off all our debts: our homes, cars, and everything else, and our most recent family vacations included Sedona, then a high-end ranch in Montana, and almost two weeks in Europe. That's all because of a big push at the beginning of my real estate career.

Since then, I've simply maintained it by working smart. Of course, I know all good things do come from the Lord, so thank you Jesus, but I've also always believed that as Ben Franklin said, "the Lord helps those who help themselves."

So, be smart and help yourself out. Most of those who are listening to this are in America. This is the land of opportunity now more than ever before. Don't listen to all those whiners and complainers… and go get you some big success.

The second thing you need to do to become a top 1% agent is…

2. Become a World-Class Real Estate Professional

You need to learn how to be a very good real estate agent, which means being a world-class expert in how to help people buy and sell homes. And that means becoming a true expert in economics, supply and demand, marketing, negotiation, project management, and logistics.

You can't just show up and be a nice, smiley person. You are asking people to pay you a lot of money to guide them through transactions often totaling in the millions of dollars, and when they ask you what to do, you need to have high-level professional answers for them.

Some brokerages will help you learn a few of the basics and leave you having to learn most of it the hard way. That makes no sense. Make sure to read my book, *The Smarter Way to Buy and Sell Your Home*, to shortcut the learning processes a ton for you.

The third thing you need to do to be a top 1% real estate agent is…

3. Fall in LOVE with Lead Generation

Once you know how to do real estate, **your #1 job is lead generation, and it always will be as long as you want to stay a top 1% real estate agent**, because no one is going to give you clients (well, there is one exception I'll describe below, and you can't be a top 1% agent if you go that route).

Right now, would be a good time to think about this: Do you want to SELL and SELL, or alternatively… **are you 100% willing to do that in order to become and stay a top 1% real estate agent?** Because that's what you will need to do consistently.

Legitimately, you might be thinking, "Well it depends what kind of selling we're talking about." I understand that…

Which brings us to the fourth thing you need to do to become a top 1% real estate agent, and that is…

4. Choose YOUR Method of Lead Generation and MASTER it.

There are ten different ways to generate leads in real estate. None of them are even remotely easy (if they were us 1% agents wouldn't make the big bucks, right?) In my opinion, there are five best ways to generate leads and five ways that are not the best. However, **any of them will work, if you invest enough time and money and trial and error into them**. Depending on your preferences, strengths, and weaknesses, some of them will instantly repel you, and you might think other methods seem like they'll be right up your alley.

The key is to pick one of those ways, maybe after a short amount of experimentation with a couple of the methods, and stick with it till you master it. Only then will that method consistently generate leads for you. You need to avoid the mistakes too many agents make of trying to do two or three approaches at a time, or continually jumping from one to another as soon as each one gets kind of challenging.

A few minutes ago I talked about how no one gives you leads, except one exception, when you join the team of a top 1% agent as a buyer's agent, and the team leader gives you some of their leads to work with. However, they aren't really giving you those leads because when they close, you'll need to give them half of the commission, and the clients, and their future business and referrals, will forever belong to the team leader, not to you.

And so, the fifth thing you need to do to become a top 1% agent is …

5. DO NOT BECOME A BUYER'S AGENT

Look, I get it, these leads can be tempting for a new agent. But here's the problem: life as a buyer's agent is tough, because you are always working, always showing homes and dealing with problems and only taking home half the money, but almost every agent who takes these leads becomes addicted.

Once you have these leads it's a hard step to walk away from them and go through the parched dry desert of learning how to get their own leads. So, you're trapped. By becoming a buyer's agent, you become dependent, and your chances of ever becoming a top 1% agent will be dramatically diminished. New agents have three possible career paths, and becoming a buyer's agent is one of them, so I recommend choosing one of the other two paths.

The sixth thing you need to do is…

6. Have a Superior Home-Selling Process and Sell It to Your Clients

Notice I didn't say a superior home selling pitch or "presentation", I said a HOME SELLING PROCESS. You need a detailed step-by-step plan for exactly how you are going to go about getting your clients the highest possible price in the shortest time for their home.

Many agents don't have an actual clue how to do this. If you think about it, the most important job of a real estate agent, the part that takes the most judgment and expertise, is helping homeowners sell their homes. Even non-real-estate agents know this, and as a result, clients are much more likely to trust a newer agent with the home-buying process than the home-selling process. If you want to be seen as a top agent and get clients to trust you with the sale of their homes, you must show them a superior home-selling process.

Do you have a top 1% home selling process? If not, study my book, *The Smarter Way to Buy and Sell Your Home*, carefully and implement the concepts described into your home selling process, and you'll be well on your way to being a top 1% real estate agent.

"If you want to be seen as a top agent and get clients to trust you with the sale of their homes, you must show them a superior home-selling process."

And finally, the seventh thing you must do to get ahead of 99% of other agents is …

7. Have A Smart Plan to Manage Your Growing Real Estate Business

I say this because when you're a 1% agent **you can't do it all by yourself for long,** and if you don't plan for the support you'll need, **I promise you'll eventually crash and experience massive burnout**, and the rewards of all your hard work will be interrupted for six months or more while you recover and pick up the pieces.

One option for organizing your business is written in detail in Gary Keller's book The Millionaire Real Estate Agent, wherein he advises you to become a manager and hire and train a team to work directly for you, and help you with client service, marketing, and paperwork. Gary's method works for some top agents, but **most agents can't stand the idea of being a manager**.

The alternative approach for top 1% agents is the method I used, which got me all the support I needed in a more flexible way, at a lower cost, and without having to become a manager, thank goodness. (There is also a third way to get support which is more suitable for those doing less business than a typical top 1% agent). In any case, see my book, *The Smarter Top Producing Real Estate Agent*, for a complete guide to all three support choices.

"When I decided to get into residential real estate, it was important for me to know I could be successful quickly. Relevate was the only firm that had systems and processes specifically designed to help new agents become top producing $10+ million-dollar agents in just a couple of years. It all made sense to me. And there were plenty of examples of other people who had followed this process and became very successful quickly, which proved it wasn't pie in the sky.

So, I had the confidence of knowing that if I did the work and I did everything that was in my control, the results were going to come. I set a super aggressive goal to sell $10 million in my first year, and I came very close, I sold $9.3 million, which made for a fantastic first year.

Now, there was an even more important factor for me. I had a young child when I started, and I didn't have any other family support here. So the biggest thing for me was that I didn't have to do it all by myself. Relevate has a support team of fully licensed agents who jump in whenever I need them, to take care of my clients to the highest standards. That was just invaluable for me.

It hurts me to know agents are at firms where there aren't solid processes, where there isn't great support. I believe in sharing good things with other people. So if any of this resonates with you, call or text me and we'll get together for coffee or a walk. I'll help you all I can, and no matter what, we'll each have made a new friend."

Ricci Treffer

Scan QR code for video

CHAPTER 5

How To Get Your First Clients in Real Estate

Scan QR code for video

I've sold over 750 homes in my career as a real estate agent. But my gosh, I still remember what it was like when

I first started and didn't even have a single client yet. It was kind of nerve wracking. So, are you ready to learn about the **top ten best tips to get your first real estate clients?** And would it be okay if this advice also helped you get your 2nd, 3rd, 4th, 10th, and 25th client? Okay, cool! Let's go!

10. Present Yourself as a Professional

Ninety percent of real estate agents dress and act way too casually. The other 10% sell 90% of homes. If you want clients to trust you and choose you and recommend you, you have to look and act like a professional. That doesn't mean you have to wear a suit, but you need to wear very nice clothes during business hours. If you don't have nice clothes, you need to buy them. If you don't know what clothes to buy, and this was me by the way, go to the right store and ask them for help. If you're a guy, that's Brooks Brothers, Jos. A. Bank or The Men's Warehouse. Our high-producing female agents recommend Banana Republic, Anne Taylor or J. Crew.

Also, speaking of being professional... be on time, check your spelling and grammar before you send an email, do what you say you are going to do, when you say you would do it. Sad to say, but doing these basic things will put you ahead of 75% of real estate agents. And that's good for you, right?

9. Know Something About Real Estate

You know by now that real estate pre-licensing classes don't teach you anything about how to help buyers and sellers, and unfortunately neither do most brokerages. But you need to know the basics about how to advise buyers and sellers, so that when someone asks you a question, you know what to say, and so you'll feel confident putting yourself out there as a real estate agent.

Luckily, we've got you covered for this. Make sure to read my book, *The Smarter Way to Buy and Sell Your Home*. In addition to that, learn how to look up data and market information in the MLS. Study those reports. Congratulations, you now know more than 80% of real estate agents. Go forth with confidence.

8. Go See People in Person and Drop Some Real Estate Knowledge on Them

Now, go see your closest friends and family in person and practice on them. Tell them the best of what you've learned. If they own a home, print out a basic CMA from MLS and show them the sale prices of the homes that have sold recently in their neighborhood.

Tell them they are hereby your first clients, not necessarily to buy or sell a home, but to be kept up to date on what's happening in the market. And, most importantly, ask them to refer you to anyone who is thinking about buying or selling a home.

Now that you've practiced with your most understanding people, go see everyone else you know, in person. Tell them you're already off to a fast start in real estate and that you already have clients you are advising. If they own a home, bring them a CMA of their neighborhood and tell them your favorite tip about increasing the value of their home (you got that from the videos I told you about a minute ago).

If they don't own a home, tell them your favorite tip about getting ready to buy a home. Then ask them if they know of anyone who is currently thinking of buying or selling a home. If they do, get the person's name and phone number and set up a time to meet with them! If they don't know anyone looking to buy, ask them to refer you to anyone they run into who is thinking about buying or selling a home.

See what we're doing here? We're not just asking people if they personally want to buy or sell. If they do, they'll know you are there to help them. We're asking them to refer us to anyone else they know of who is thinking about buying or selling a home. That gets you exposed to many more potential clients. And we're only on the 3rd idea to get clients. You're doing great so far!

7. Put Everyone You Meet into a Database Management System

You need to keep track of the contact information of everyone you talk to about real estate, including their phone, email, and home address at a minimum, along with a record of your interactions with them. I actually don't know of any good database management systems for realtors. I don't like any of them. At the very least you could use a spreadsheet for this.

At Relevate we programmed our own database system from scratch to do exactly what we want it to do, and we love it. But it's only available to Relevate agents.

Now here is the key... everyone you meet who has told you they'd recommend you needs to go into this system, and from now on, until the end of your ridiculously successful real estate career many years from now, you need to send everyone in that database something related to real estate every month, and call them to follow up and ask them if they've run into anyone who is thinking about buying or selling a home. Otherwise, they won't remember to refer you. It's your job to remind them, to keep yourself at the top of their mind.

Next, while you're out there talking to everyone you know, it's super important that you also...

6. Talk To New People

Here's the deal... half of the people you knew before getting into real estate will support you and refer you... eventually. They all know tons of people who got into real estate and then quit after a few months. They also know you just started in real estate recently, so many of them will want to know you've gained some real-world experience before recommending you. So, for those reasons, you'll need to prove the real estate part of you before they trust you.

The other half of the people who knew you before you got into real estate will have a really hard time seeing you as a real estate professional at all. They knew you as what you were before real estate and that's the picture they have in their mind about you, regardless of what you do.

For these reasons, you need to meet new people who didn't know you before you got into real estate. These new people will know you only as a real estate agent, and that's a big advantage. Three points here:

1. **Do not attend traditional networking events.** You won't have anything in common with them except needing business. Those relationships are going nowhere. You need to think about what you enjoy doing and go do it with other people who enjoy the same thing. Join a chess or ping pong club or volunteer at a museum or a political campaign. My best places for meeting people were at church and CrossFit.

2. **Each time you attend an event, make it a goal to meet two or three new people.** Ask them what they do for a living, then they'll ask you, and you can ask them if they know a real estate agent they feel comfortable referring to friends and family. If they don't, tell them you'd like to earn their trust to be that person. And that leads to our third super important point...

3. Believe what I'm about to tell you because it's true. **More people than you think will use you as a realtor or refer to you as their friend, even if they just met you.** My friend Wendy, in Dallas, Texas, started in real estate after a stellar 20-year career as a stay-at-home mom. 95% of the people she knew before real estate only knew her as a mom, and none of them sent her any business. Almost everyone who did were people she didn't know before she got into real estate. She sold 51 homes in her first year.

You do not have to have helped a person buy or sell a home, for that person to recommend you. You just must make a good impression and follow up. Which is why I recommend not carrying business cards with you because you'll ...

5. Send Handwritten Personal Notes in Hand-Addressed Envelopes

... with your business card inside it, which will give you a good excuse to ask the person for their home address, right? People just don't receive handwritten personal notes anymore, and that will make you stand out as a special and thoughtful person who follows up as promised. And of course, you'll be smart and get nice heavy solid magnetic cards because it makes you seem more substantial and like you believe in yourself enough to invest 25 cents per card instead of 2 cents. People throw paper cards away, but they put magnetic cards on their fridges or filing cabinets where they'll see them every day.

Make it a habit to send hand-written notes after each time you speak with anyone about real estate.

You'll also have created Facebook, Instagram, and LinkedIn social media accounts, and friended everyone you meet, because that's how you'll...

4. Show Everyone Evidence of You Being Busy Doing Real Estate

You might say "Mike, I have no clients, so how can I do this?" Here's how…

First, get it into your head that "client" doesn't necessarily mean a person who is buying or selling a home with you right this minute. A client is anyone who sees you as their source of real estate information and to whom you are regularly supplying real estate information. And you're currently doing that for everyone you've put into your database, right? Yes, you are.

Next, schedule previews of listings in every part of the city or towns near you and take pictures and videos of you doing it. Post these images on social media, point out the homes you like the most for your clients and why, and talk and write about the advantages and features of each part of the city and each town. Also, volunteer to show homes and do open houses for other agents who are too busy to handle everything on their own and take pictures and videos of you doing that, too.

"You do not need to have helped a person buy or sell a home for that person to recommend you. You just must make a good impression and follow up."

All this will show people how busy you are, and you'll get educated about the market more than many busy agents. The bottom line is that only 1 in 100 agents will actually do this advice. I don't know why. But you are a go-getter, and people will notice all this activity and begin to believe in you BIG TIME. Soon, you'll be busy with people who want to buy and sell now.

Okay, we've arrived at our top three tips for getting your first clients in real estate, and tip #3 is...

3. Be a Leader and Organizer

When people choose a realtor, they want a leader. Someone to take charge and make things happen for them. So, you need to be seen as a leader in other parts of your life too. This will supercharge your efforts to get people to trust you and recommend you.

For example, in every group I was a part of, I put together a membership directory to help people get to know each other, what they did for a living, their hobbies, and if they had a spouse and kids. Everyone loved it, and I got to know them and get their contact information. Almost all of them subsequently used me to buy or sell their home or recommended me to others.

One very powerful specific way to be a leader and be seen as a proactive value-adding person is to...

2. Knock on Every Door Around You and Build a Vendor List

Start with whatever neighborhood is nearest to you. Print out multiple copies of two things before you leave home: CMAs from MLS for that neighborhood, and a basic list of vendors who you feel confident recommending that homeowners normally need: HVAC services, lawn service, electrician, plumber, etc. If you don't have a decent list, ask other agents in your office, they'll have tons of recommendations.

Go out on a Saturday or after work and knock on each door and say something like, "Hi, I'm Suzy Smith, I live around the corner, and I'm a real estate agent. I wanted to give you this analysis of our neighborhood, and also this list of vendors I recommend who you might need someday. And I wanted to ask you if you knew any really great vendors I should add to this list, like [and then name five or six categories you don't have yet, like computer repair, carpenter, painter, countertop installer, hardwood floor refinisher, accountant, appliance repair, favorite restaurants, you get the idea].

Either they'll engage with you or they won't. If they do great. Add their suggestions to the list and ask them if they've run into anyone who is thinking about buying or selling a home. Add them to your database or spreadsheet, and mail them the updated and expanded vendor list. They'll love it because they helped you make that list. They're already on your team.

Again, most agents won't do this type of thing. You will and you'll get the business. People want to work with and recommend a leader, a go-getter. This is an outstanding example of what that looks like.

And finally, the #1 way to get your first client is to…

1. Seek to Be Respected, Not Liked

At this point, before even considering doing anything I'm recommending in this blog, I urge you to ask yourself the question that will define your career… "Do you care more about being respected, or liked?"

Here's the deal, if you care most about being respected, you might still be nervous about doing what I'm recommending here, but you'll do it because you care more about being successful, than about what people think of you. And people will notice you doing things to be successful that they themselves are afraid to do, and that will cause them to respect you, and that in turn will cause most of them to sincerely like you.

The number one thing you need to do to be successful in real estate is to ask for business. You need to ask and ask and ask. If you don't ask, you won't get it. And if you care more about being liked than you care about your own success … you won't ask.

If you care most about being liked, you'll be constantly worried about what people are thinking about you when you are doing the admittedly gutsy things I recommend in this chapter. You'll have a stomachache during every minute of it and you won't ask for business like you need to. You'll be so worried about bugging people that you'll be apologizing all the time.

Successful real estate agents are leaders who make things happen. They understand the importance of being successful, not just for their own personal ambitions, but because the world needs leaders who are willing to put themselves out there to accomplish big goals for the benefit of everyone around them.

So, are your goals important enough not to care what other people think as you go after them? If so, everything I've recommended in this chapter will help you achieve those goals sooner rather than later.

How to Get Your Next 100 Clients

I've got one more powerful technique you should use. In addition to continuing all that I've explained in this chapter so far, this is the most important technique to get your next 100 or 1000 clients.

When you've done a great job for a client, get a photo of them with the sold sign (and you can do that for buyers too). Interview them and write up their words of praise for you, and plaster that testimonial everywhere. This is called evidence of success. Many of your people will be waiting to see if you actually sell a house before they'll go out on a limb to recommend you. So, show them!

As I said earlier, you need to be consistent with sending real estate information out to your database and following up to ask for business. At Relevate Real Estate, we have tons of systems to make all this easier, smoother, and lower cost.

"As a new agent, my first priority was to get complete and thorough training about how to do real estate right, because honestly... I'm not one that likes to make mistakes and serving my clients well is my first priority. Second, I wanted to get on my feet quickly as a self-sufficient business owner and get this thing started.

So I interviewed a number of firms, and what impressed me was a couple of things. First, Relevate had better training than anyone else offered.

Other firms were like, "we'll be here if you need us". That's not what I needed. Relevate had a thorough and detailed training program, and a very-available and attentive broker-in-charge. I got all the knowledge I needed, and was fully supported.

Second, I saw a lot of people like me at Relevate who had become top-producing agents, and heard about the life-balance they all had, which was NOT AT ALL what I expected to hear. I'll be really honest, during my interview when they talked about ME becoming a top producing agent, I was very wide-eyed. I looked at them and said, "I'd love to get there, but that's really far away in my mind, it's not where I envision being anytime soon."

Nineteen months later, I was there. I had sold $10 million in a 12-month period. It was crazy. Honestly, never my wildest dreams. And it's just gotten better since.

The Relevate system works. But you've got to have the discipline to really do the work, to dig in and do it 100%."

Tara Franco

Scan QR code for video

CHAPTER 6

The Five BEST Ways to Get Clients in Real Estate

Scan QR code for video

To help our agents here at Relevate be as efficient and successful as possible, we've scientifically studied all the ways residential real estate agents have ever tried to get clients. This chapter is about **the five best ways to generate leads**... four ways that are pretty darn good and **one way that blows every other approach out of the water**. So, if you want to know how to get clients in the most efficient ways, you are in the right place.

Before we start, I'll tell you two things:

First, I have personally tried every one of the five worst and five best methods on my way to selling over 750 homes in my 17-year career, so I'm sharing real-life experience here.

Second, my background before real estate was in operations research and process improvement, applying math and science to business. In fact, I wrote two books* on the subject. Our analysis of the worst five and best five ways to generate leads in real estate was not based on opinion, it was based on calculating the return-on-investment of each method ... in other words, we compared the time and money agents must invest, versus the take-home income the agents receive, using each method.

Let's jump in. The least awesome of the five best ways to generate leads in residential real estate is only for hard-core salespeople, but it can generate business, and that is...

5. Cold Calling For-Sale-By-Owners and Expired Listings

This strategy isn't for everyone because most people don't enjoy cold calling. Especially calling people who either think they don't need a real estate agent (in the case of FSBOs) or who have just recently been disappointed by an agent (in the case of expired listings).

However, these are sellers who want to sell. It's easy to get these lists to call, there's great software to help you make these calls, and there are tons of great strategies and scripts you can use to help you be effective at this strategy. You just must be the type of person who can make yourself sit down and do it.

When a client with an expired listing says, "My last agent only charged 4%," I like to hit them with this: "Okay, but they didn't sell your home, right? So if you could go back and agree to 6% to get it sold in two weeks, would you do it?" Nine times out of ten, they'll say, "Well, yeah."

That's when I follow up with, "Great—now you have that chance."

It's a simple way to show them the real value of working with an agent who can actually close the deal.

Many agents have built their businesses by using the 4th best way to generate leads…

4. Hosting Open Houses

In some markets, open houses are very popular, whereas in other markets open houses are rare. They are fairly rare in our area. However, they can still be very effective if you choose the right ones (which means above-average price ranges and lots of traffic) and market and manage them using the best possible approaches.

To get these opportunities, I suggest you market yourself as the "Open House Agent" to other agents in your firm, and even make a brochure other agents can use to sell your Open House services to their sellers. You may even be able to do Open Houses for agents at other firms, if the right agency paperwork is signed and permissions are granted.

Open houses certainly take a lot of time, and mostly on weekends. But there is no doubt they can be effective for agents to meet new buyers.

The 3rd best way to get clients in residential real estate is called…

3. Farming

Farming is also known as "Neighborhood Targeting". This means choosing a neighborhood and mailing to and interacting with everyone in it regularly, showing your real estate ability and demonstrating specific knowledge of the neighborhood from your research. The idea is to work hard and consistently to get a few home sales in the neighborhood and position yourself as the obvious choice for any homeowner who is thinking about selling.

Meeting you in person will multiply the effectiveness of this strategy ten-fold, so I would absolutely add door knocking to this strategy. This involves going door to door with some small gift, like a nicely-printed recommended vendor list, and asking homeowners who else they recommend, and then mailing the new list to everyone you visit.

I also recommend making videos showing your knowledge and insights about the neighborhood's sales history, and sending postcards with QR codes to residents so they can easily watch the video. You'll also need a nice webpage for people to visit when they consider interviewing you to sell their home.

We've now arrived at the top two ways to generate leads in residential real estate. Our research revealed that the 2nd best method of getting clients is…

2. Social Media

Using social media for lead generation can work reasonably well. Level one is to post consistent and professional images of yourself and your real estate ability, mostly on Facebook and Instagram.

"You can work by referral as a brand-new agent."

By far the most important posts will be testimonials from happy clients with photographs of those happy clients standing near your sold sign (whether they were the buyer or seller), because their photo shows first that the testimonial is very real, and second that the clients are 100% putting their personal stamp of approval on you.

Level two of the social media strategy is short videos and reels on YouTube, Facebook, and Instagram. These don't take much effort and will really help people know you better. Level three is long-form videos on YouTube… These take another level of equipment and editing but can be very effective.

One point to consider here… don't feel you need to create any branding for yourself beyond your name and your beautiful face. It will cost you time and money and will actually hurt more than help (regardless of what branding experts say). I go more in-depth on personal branding in my book, *The Smarter Top Producing Real Estate Agent.*

We have now arrived at what our research conclusively proved to be **the most efficient lead generation method in residential real estate** by a wide margin over every other method, including the second-place method, social media. And the #1 method of generating leads is...

1. Working By Referral

This is the method for which we've developed extensive systems and support at Relevate Real Estate. Because when we compare the time and money agents need to invest in this method to the take-home income results, it just blows away every other method of lead generation for residential real estate agents.

A big point to understand is that there is a very big difference between doing business by "word of mouth," which means "doing a great job and hoping people refer" versus "working by referral," which means "doing a great job and teaching and reminding people to refer." That's a 5x difference in terms of the results you get.

Another key point is that you do not need to have done any real estate work for a person for that person to be willing to refer you. If you do this approach right, you'll get just as many referrals from people you've never worked with as from people you have worked with.

That means you can work by referral as a brand-new agent. There will be a lot of work to do to build your initial sphere of influence, but we teach agents how to do that all the time, and while it's not easy, it's doable.

The steps to success working by referral are:

First, qualify people to be on your referral team by explaining to them that you do business by referral and asking if they would be willing to refer you.

Second, send these referral team members marketing material each month showing your character and competence. At Relevate, we develop these campaigns for our agents because, why not? If they all need to send something really good each month, why not share the cost and effort of planning, designing, and printing? Of the twelve campaigns, two normally take the form of in-person events, and two are small gifts hand-delivered to the clients' homes by either their agent or our team.

Third, call behind the marketing material to say "Hi" and ask for referrals.

Fourth, send hand-written personal notes after each conversation.

In addition, we support our agents to incorporate social media as an "icing on the cake" to stay in touch and remind people of how good they are at real estate and that they love referrals. However, it is surprising how many of our agents are super successful doing business by referral, and hardly ever post anything on social media.

The Five BEST Ways to Get Clients

"Out of all the firms I interviewed with as a newly licensed agent, Relevate was the only one that could actually lay out a path of training for me in a way that I could understand, and know I was going to get the support, help and training that I needed.

Everyone else SAID they had a path, but really couldn't give me details. I would ask questions and they would be very vague.

Relevate was very clear, "Here is the exact plan, here is exactly what you need to do."

I'm a checklist type person, and that's what I was looking for.

Another big deal for me was broker-in-charge support. Many of these firms had one BIC for over a hundred agents, and when I asked about availability they wouldn't give me a straight answer. The BIC at Relevate said "That's my job, you can call me anytime for help." And that turned out to be 100% true. I always had help literally within minutes of asking.

Then, pretty much immediately after I arrived, I was introduced to my mentor, Tara, who was perfect for me. She helped me more than I can express, and she's become a great friend. All that added up to a great start for me.

I closed $8.4 million in volume my first full year, and I'm over $10 million in volume in this slow market, even though I hear most agents are down 30%.

So, I am grateful. And I want every new agent to enjoy the kind of start I had. I'd be happy to share the details of my experience with you and answer your questions. Just text or call me and we'll get together and talk."

Brandie Upshaw

Scan QR code for video

CHAPTER 7

The Five WORST Ways to Get Clients in Real Estate

Scan QR code for video

Now that we've discussed the five best ways to get clients, this chapter is about the five worst possible ways to get clients as a real estate agent, but lots of agents still use these methods. I don't know why. So, if you want to know which ways to avoid getting clients and being inefficient, you are in the right place. Let's go...

5. Specialize in a Niche

Many agents feel that specializing will make them more attractive to clients in that niche market. Common examples are divorce (because usually it involves a sale and two purchases and there is some common legal knowledge an educated agent can bring), or luxury homes (because they sell for high prices). Other niches are downtown condos, police, teachers and firefighters, seniors, certain ethnic groups or languages.

The upside of this strategy is that the agent is building their own lead generation pipeline. The downside is that in general we've observed that almost all niches in residential real estate are too narrow: this strategy will tend to push more clients away (the majority who aren't in your chosen niche and think you don't want to help them) than it attracts.

In our experience, residential real estate in a certain broad geographical area is as tight of a niche as you need to or want to be in. We definitely recommend writing blogs or making videos showing off your knowledge about any specific niche, but it probably doesn't make sense to tell the market you are limited to only helping a certain narrow group of clients.

The second least-worst method of getting clients in real estate can actually be a great way to start – but only if you do it right. If so, this method actually could move over to being in the top five best methods to generate leads. Unfortunately, two-thirds of agents do it wrong, which is why it's here on this list. And that is…

4. Buying Leads Generated By Someone Else

There are three types of leads agents commonly buy from someone else. In these cases you don't own the source of the leads and you could be cut off, or the deal could be changed, at any time. And that does happen, usually by surprise. The other factor is that almost all of these leads are buyer leads, not seller leads.

The Five WORST Ways to Get Clients

The first type of buying leads from someone else is...

A. Buying Leads from Zillow or Realtor.com or OpCity

Or any one of 50 different websites that capture leads and sell them to real estate agents. The big benefit of these services is instant leads. You just pay for the lead and you get it instantly. These leads cost anywhere from $60 to $500 each, so that's a little expensive, and that wouldn't be so bad if they converted to clients and closings at a higher rate. That's the difficult part.

Allow me to share some numbers with you. Last year these sites combined sold a total of 50 million leads to agents… but there were only a little over five million homes actually sold. So 10 leads get one sale, right? wrong. Because 80% of those sold homes, or four million out of five million, were sold to buyers who either got their agent by referral or who bought with an onsite new construction agent.

So, only one million homes were sold from the 50 million leads given to agents, so for all leads sold to agents, only 1 in 50 actually closed. So the low conversion rate is the challenging part of buying these leads. Every year more leads are sold to agents, but the total number of homes sold doesn't increase at nearly the same rate.

As a result, you could spend a lot of time and money on leads and work really hard on each of them, but not close enough to make financial sense.

The second way to get buyer leads that someone else has generated is by...

B. Working as Buyer's Agent for a Busy Team Leader

In this case, you are buying leads from the team leader by promising to serve them in exchange for giving up about half the commission. These clients belong to the team leader, so you won't be able to build your own business based on the relationships you build with them.

Being a buyer's agent is a way to get busy in real estate, but you'll be working very hard for the money you earn and becoming more dependent on the team leader instead of building a business of your own.

And the third way to buy leads from someone else who generates them is...

"Being a buyer's agent is a way to get busy in real estate, but you'll be working very hard for the money you earn and becoming more dependent on the team leader instead of building a business of your own."

C. Receiving Relocation Leads from Your Brokerage

When you accept relocation leads from your brokerage, you'll be lucky to receive 30% of the commission. That's because the relocation company normally keeps over 40% of the commission, and your firm will usually keep 30%+ for handing the lead to you. That adds up to a lot of commission you won't be getting, in exchange for a ton of work by you. And relocation leads often keep you disproportionately busy on weekends because that's when they are normally free to visit their new hometown.

So why is this method ranked slightly better than being a buyer's agent on a team? Because these clients normally belong to you after they close, so you have the opportunity to stay in touch with them and earn referrals and repeat business; and these relocation buyers tend to be at higher price ranges.

Concluding Thoughts About Buying Leads

Okay, now I'll explain what I mean by one-third of agents doing this right and benefiting from buying leads, and two-thirds not. The agents who do it right build strong relationships with the clients who belong to them (in the case of relocation and leads purchased from websites), and those clients become their database from which to build their own independent referral lead flow.

One of our best and consistently highest-producing agents did just this. She started with Zillow leads and built solid relationships with every client, even if they weren't ready to buy a home right away. Soon she had enough referral business from those leads to not pay for Zillow leads ever again, and she's never looked back.

Unfortunately, the biggest problem I've consistently seen with two-thirds of agents who buy leads (whether they pay per lead up front or pay at closing by giving up a big part of the commission) is that they get addicted to the ease of these instant leads and completely stop doing anything else. They've got enough clients to take care of that they're not desperate, and as a result, they aren't willing to go through the pain of learning to generate their own leads.

So over time they get more and more dependent on someone else, and they never grow their own business. Good enough substitutes for potentially great in their careers and in their lives, and I think that's a bummer.

The next terrible way to generate leads is…

3. Short Sale and REO Specialization

In a slower market there are opportunities for agents to specialize in handling Short Sales, or selling REO (which stands for "Real Estate Owned") properties for banks. These methods of getting business have four big disadvantages:

1. No one involved is having a good time. It's all very depressing.

2. Banks don't like paying commission to real estate agents and they will cut you coming and going.

3. You have to deal with a ton of slow bank bureaucracy that you'll swear makes no sense.

4. These methods only work in down markets, so when the market is good, this method to get business is pretty useless.

So in our opinion, this method of getting business should only be a last resort. I'd quit real estate before doing this.

The almost most terrible way to generate leads is...

2. Direct Marketing

This comes in two forms: digital in the form of emails or texts, or regular mail, normally in the form of postcards. You would think email would be close to free, but to do it right, you need to buy lists and pay for a service to send them to avoid having your address automatically marked as spam by the receiving servers.

Normal mail is very expensive. You've got to cover the costs of copywriting, design, printing, and postage. These direct marketing methods usually deliver exactly zero results, and even when you get a few responses, when you compare the costs to the benefits, this method just doesn't cut it.

And finally, we've reached the very worst ever way to generate leads in real estate, and that is...

1. Advertising

This includes both online advertising, which includes Search Engine Optimization (SEO) on your own website, banner ads, pay-per-click on google, and running ads on sites like Facebook and LinkedIn; and also traditional media such as billboards, radio, and print publications.

The bottom line regarding this type of lead generation is that it is very expensive, it generates very few leads, and the leads it generates are strangers with whom you have no basis of trust. In the end, it is almost impossible to not lose tons of money trying to use this method to generate buyer and seller leads.

Which Lead Generation Method is Best for YOUR Business?

"Before joining Relevate Real Estate, I was at three different brokerages, including one big national brand-name firm. They were all very nice people, but none of them really had any systems or processes for a new agent to follow. You were pretty much on your own to figure out how to get clients and how to and oh, what should I do? Which is why I wasn't getting the business I should have been getting.

Then I heard about Relevate Real Estate from a friend who is a very successful agent there. And WOW it was a completely different world compared to anywhere else. Relevate is truly a process improvement company, that happens to do real estate.

So for me, they actually had just what I was looking for, an entire system that tells me what activities to do every day, a point system that tells me when I've won each day, and proof that if you keep winning days consistently, you'll have tons of clients consistently. And... it actually works! I've got three pendings already for this month, and I'm super motivated to just keep working the system, because I KNOW it works and I

KNOW my business will just keep growing, which obviously is super exciting.

I want other agents to know about Relevate because real estate can be a real struggle. I want to see other agents have the tools I have now, right from the start. Just give me a call and I'd love to get coffee and sit down and tell you about it and answer your questions."

Kristy Buschhorn

Scan QR code for video

CHAPTER 8

Three TERRIBLE Career-Crushing Mistakes Real Estate Agents Make When Growing Their Business

Scan QR code for video

I wrote this chapter because I made many of the mistakes I'll be discussing and I want to save you from experiencing the pain I went through. The biggest mistake agents make when growing their business is to be dependent on someone else for leads. This is a problem for a lot of reasons.

1. Being Dependent On Someone Else For Your Leads

First, because in fact by doing this, you are not growing your own business but instead you're working hard to grow the business of the lead supplier, which is to make money from you by selling you leads... or getting referral fees from the leads they give you, which is the same thing, you're just paying a lot more after closing on closed leads, instead of paying less per lead up front.

The second reason this is a problem for your career is that the supplier of those leads could cut you off at any time for any reason.

And the third reason is that you're incurring lead purchase expenses that on average, compared to working to build your own lead generation system, reduce your take home income by about 50%. You might say, "Well it's worth it because I didn't have to go get the leads myself. Well, no, that's BS for two reasons…

> (a) because you could get those leads yourself for a lot less, even taking the value of your time into account, and

> (b) you are not considering that the leads you get from someone else are usually low quality and require so much of your time to convert into a closing. And that if you used that same amount of time and effort to get higher quality leads for yourself, you'd end up spending the same amount of time to both get and convert the lead, and not have to pay for the lead in the first place.

This mistake even applies to established agents who have a good amount of leads coming in from their own efforts, who drop everything and gladly agree to take a referral from another agent with a 25% referral fee or from a relocation company with a (gulp) 42% referral fee. The time the agent spends serving that client and getting paid much less than normal could have been invested in getting several more clients on which the agent could have kept their full normal commission.

Finally, the biggest problem I've seen with this mistake is that two-thirds of those who take these kinds of leads get addicted to them, and simply stop even trying to build their own independent businesses, even though they are working all the time and never truly get ahead financially. As a result, they never have enough money to reinvest in a support team to free them up to get even more business while also having a balanced life.

The solution is to invest your unpaid time up front to create your own lead flow. Yes, I know this requires delayed gratification, not getting something immediately after you do a little work, but that's the nature of building your own business, and really the nature of success in life in general.

Your job is lead generation. That's the most valuable activity in your business. Henry Ford once said, "Nothing happens until someone sells something." That's got to be you for your business. You need to own and control your source of business, otherwise you are working for someone else, the person or company who is generating those leads.

I've analyzed all the different ways real estate agents generate leads for themselves. Don't spread yourself too thin. Pick one of those methods and master it. None of them are easy. All these methods work, but they all take time and effort to make them work for you consistently. If you dedicate yourself to mastery of your chosen lead generation method, you will own your source of lead generation and you will be the master of your own business.

2. Not Marketing To Your Past Clients

The next big mistake is always chasing new lead sources and strangers and not keeping in touch with past clients and asking them for referrals.

Your past clients won't refer you to others, if you don't stay top of their minds and actually ask them to do so.

Not staying in touch with past clients is a problem because they are your best source of business. 80% of buyers and sellers find their agent by referral. Your past clients want to refer you. Their friends are asking which agent they use and because you aren't keeping in touch they can't remember your name or your number! If you do a really good job of staying in touch with past clients, eventually you won't need any other types of lead generation.

The solution is to have a system to keep in touch with past clients. To do this you'll need a marketing program. At least every 45 days, you need to send something to all your past clients that they'll think is cool. It could be about real estate, like a report of what's happening in the market. Or it could be an invitation to a happy hour you are hosting for them. Either way, whatever you send is simply this: it's an excuse to call them and say "hi". It's something you are giving them, so you can feel good about asking them if they know anyone who is thinking about buying or selling. You don't get if you don't ask. My friend Tim says "No asky, no getty."

You'll need to have a good database system to keep their names and contact information, birthdays and closing anniversaries, reminders to call for all kinds of other reasons, all their transaction records, and notes about your interactions with them. It will also really help if the software allows you to prioritize people based on how likely they are to refer, and to be able to group them, like which of them are moms so you can deliver a

Mother's Day gift to them, or who's into college football or girls nights out with wine.

One reason some agents hesitate to touch base with past clients is they're worried they might be upset with them about something that happened during the transaction. That's a pretty common fear. I've even thought this at times when I was a busy agent. Sometimes, yes, a client was emotional during or right after a transaction but it's crazy how it's like childbirth, they might be feeling pain during it, but right after they forget the pain and they love you. In my experience, 90% of the time when you think they're mad at you they'll surprise you with expressions of joy and love when you call.

That's real estate for you. You've got nothing to lose by making that call and saying "hello".

3. Reducing your listing commission

The third big mistake agents make while trying to grow their business is reducing their listing commission.

Doing this is a big problem. Again, for several reasons.

"Henry Ford once said, 'Nothing happens until someone sells something.'

Your job is lead generation. That's the most valuable activity in your business."

First by discounting your commission, you are telling the client you don't respect the value you bring, and that client will never again respect you or your advice as much as they originally would have, and that will make you less effective for them.

Second, by discounting your commission, you are telling them you're a bad negotiator, and that when a buyer's agent brings an offer, you'll give away the price of their home also. After all, the seller's reason, if you give away your own money right in front of them, for sure you'll give away their money when they aren't watching you.

Third, let's use 6% total commission as an example because that's the minimum our agents are worth at Relevate based on the value we bring to sellers. 3% goes to the buyer's agent, so you're left with 3%. If you give up 1% of your commission, that reduces your revenue by 33%, not 1%. For the average agent, that's half of what's left over after all expenses, profit, meaning you've just cut your take-home income in half. And that's when you only give away 1%.

Finally, once an agent starts doing this, it's hard to stop.

Remember earlier we talked about getting referrals from your past clients? ... Now when they refer you, they'll tell the new client, "Hey, they'll reduce their commission, just ask." And you'll have to because after all, you did it for their friend. Now you HAVE to do it for them, too.

The solution is to have value to offer sellers and be able to explain it clearly and in a compelling way.

Sellers want to sell their home fast and for the maximum price. How exactly do you deliver that for sellers? If you aren't sure, then study the home selling process and come up with a process or system you believe in for them.

Next, realize that at least half the time when a seller asks you to reduce your commission, they're just asking. If you say no, these people will say "Okay, I was just asking, where do I sign?" They were testing you, and although they won't admit it, they're relieved you said "no". They understand that if you stand up for your own value, you'll also stand up for the value of their home. Right?

Finally, you've got to accept that there are just some cheap people out there that don't appreciate value no matter how you or anyone else explains it. They know everything, trust no one, and will always go with the cheapest choice and get the cheapest results no matter what.

As a business owner, you need to tell yourself "Not all business is good business" and walk away. Working for these types of people is a nightmare anyway. Let another agent deal with them. If you drop your commission enough to make these people happy, you'll drown your self-respect, and the future of your business, with it.

Conclusion

These are three terrible mistakes I see agents making daily and the solutions to those mistakes so you can escape them… Or hey, hopefully never make them in the first place.

I was pretty blunt in my explanations because I don't want you or your family to suffer from the consequences of making those terrible mistakes. I want you to have everything this great business can give you, without unnecessary pain and suffering.

Three Terrible Career-Crushing Mistakes

"I was stuck at $3-4 million in volume for years. Here's how I broke through to $17 million. My first year in real estate I was rookie of the year. But after that for years I was stuck at 3-4 million in volume. I was constantly trying different things. I didn't have any plan at all, no system for what to do or when to do it. I was frustrated. I was exhausted. And to be honest, I was thinking "should I even be an agent?"

Finally a few years ago I heard about the system I'm using now, totally different from anything I'd done before. I met "normal" people who did this system and went from zero or wherever they were stuck at, to 10 million, 15 million, 25 million in volume in just a couple years. And I was like, wow, If they can do it, I can do it, one hundred percent. And sure enough, I went from nothing to $17 million in volume, it seemed like overnight.

It's a different world for me now. I know if I just do the system, I'll be fine. It just takes away so much of the stress I was feeling before. The system is just simple, and I think brilliant. Everything is gamified and measurable, you know exactly what to do each day, and when I'm done, I relax and do what I want, knowing I did what I needed to do for that day. All the marketing is planned and tested in advance, and you have a licensed support team to help you take great care of clients without having to build your own team.

Listen, I remember feeling lost and that the business wasn't working for me, and I should do something else. I know how hard that is. I think I have a responsibility to help other people get out of that place and into something much better. So, I want to share this system with you. If you're curious, give me a call or text. We'll grab a coffee or a zoom and I'll tell you all about it."

Chuck Belden

Scan QR code for video

CHAPTER 9

Three HORRIBLE Business-Destroying Mistakes Agents Make When Growing Their Business

Scan QR code for video

Hopefully, you'll be able to avoid the terrible mistakes we discussed previously. In this chapter, we'll discuss three more horrible mistakes we hope you can avoid, and the first one is…

1. Giving buyer rebates

The first mistake some agents make, and this may be the worst of all the terrible and horrible mistakes, is to give Buyer Rebates. This means to give part of your commission to the buyer as an incentive to use you.

This is the same as discounting your listing commission, as we discussed in our previous terrible mistakes chapter, except it's even worse because normally buyers don't even pay commissions! The listing agent normally pays the buyer's agent out of the commission they receive from the seller. So, the buyer isn't even really getting a rebate because they didn't pay anything. It's just a bribe from the agent!

And again, just like discounting your listing commission, after you do it, the buyer won't respect you or listen to your advice. After all, by doing this you are showing a big lack of respect for your own profession and your own abilities.

Next, you're demonstrating your lack of negotiating ability. After all, if you'll give up your own family's money so easily while your client is right there watching you, your client can only assume you'll give up their money while they're not watching, and you are negotiating on their behalf.

Also, you're giving up a huge part of your take-home income. After all, if you give your client 1% of the purchase price of the home, you are giving away 33% of the 3% commission, which for most agents is equal to half of their take-home income after all expenses.

Finally, once you start this, it's almost impossible to stop. When you get referred by past clients, the referrer will say, "You should use this agent, they'll give you part of their commission!" Then you'll be forced to give the rebate because after all, you gave it to their friend, and now you have to give it to them. You don't want that to be you.

"Oh, but Mike if I don't give a rebate I won't have that client and one client is better than no clients." Here's the solution for that. Stop giving away your commissions immediately. Then you'll need half as many clients and therefore use up half as much time serving clients to make the same money.

Then, you can invest the time you saved into getting good at getting more clients. And you'll get ahead faster. You just need to believe in yourself and the value you bring. Look back to chapter 6, choose one of the best ways to get clients, master it, and you'll be way better off.

The solution for this HORRIBLE mistake is the same as the fix for discounting your listing commission. Explain, in a compelling way, how you help buyers find the home they will love, negotiate a great price, and make sure they aren't getting stuck with a lemon. If they don't want to pay you, walk away and let another agent experience the joy of working with them.

2. Not having a CRM

The second horrible mistake agents make is not having their past clients and sphere of influence in good Customer Relationship Management (CRM) software. It blows my mind when people join our brokerage, that most of them don't have any kind of organized list of their clients. Most of the time it's just the contacts on their phone.

This is a problem because your past clients and sphere of influence is the single most valuable asset you have as a real estate agent. And as we discussed in the previous chapter, it's a terrible mistake not to stay in touch with them. Over 75% of clients find their agent by referral, and you are the one they'll refer... if they can remember your name. You can't call and remind them unless you have a way of remembering their names and contact information.

The solution is to have a decent CRM! Even a spreadsheet would be better than what most agents have, but really you want a CRM that supports the way YOU work. Most real estate CRMs, like KVCore and LionDesk, are mostly designed to manage cold leads (either purchased directly or through advertising) and distribute them to buyers' agents. That's not what you need, unless you are making terrible mistake #1, being dependent on others for your leads.

The main point of having a CRM is to cultivate referrals from your past clients and sphere of influence. And for that you need to have a database system that keeps relationship-oriented information like birthdays, closing anniversaries, hobbies, and notes from your conversations with them.

We could not find a database that did this well, so we developed our own software at Relevate which is designed 100% to support working by referral. However, if you aren't an agent at Relevate, my best recommendation is ReferralMaker CRM from Buffini & Company. It's $49 per month and totally worth it to have a solid CRM.

3. Being on the "Client Service vs Marketing Roller Coaster"

The final mistake agents make as they work to grow their businesses is actually the normal way most agents do business. This is called "being on the Client Service v Marketing Roller Coaster". These agents are either completely focused on serving their current clients, or they don't have any because they neglected to keep marketing while they were seving their clients.

Then they stress out, and worry about their bleak-looking future, and throw together a random marketing effort. They do just enough to get a few more clients and then they again switch over to focusing 100% of their attention on them.

This is a big problem for several reasons:

First, it's stressful to always be worried about where your next client will come from.

Second, these agents always have not enough, or just enough clients to get by. Because that's all they can handle at one time. They get overwhelmed quickly because there's a lot to do in a real estate transaction and they are doing it all themselves.

They never experience an abundance of business because they can't handle abundance. Therefore, there is no getting ahead; there is only scrambling and surviving as the roller coaster goes up and down, up and down.

And so, these agents might get by, but their growth is capped.

But there is an even bigger issue with this situation. These agents don't have enough clients to have choices. Since they always have barely enough or not enough clients, they can't afford to say "NO" to any of them. They need them all.

"It blows my mind when people join our brokerage, that most of them don't have any kind of organized list of their clients."

And that tempts them, or in their minds sometimes forces them, to compromise and make many of the terrible and horrible mistakes we are warning you against. Things like giving up your commission and buying leads. And of course that makes everything worse.

Having enough clients to have choices is the key to happiness and success in real estate. But if you're doing everything in your business by yourself, you don't have the capacity to have enough clients to have choices. And that's a tricky situation to be in.

The solution for this mistake is to have knowledgeable, reliable, solid, affordable, licensed agents on your team that you can trust to help you serve your clients.

And the arrangement needs to be that you pay them when they are needed, and you don't have to pay them when you don't need them.

The way you'll work with these wonderful team members is that you won't hand the clients off to them, you'll work together with them to help your clients, like a doctor and a nurse or physician's assistant, each doing

Three Horrible Business-Destroying Mistakes

your role to take great care of your client. Clients love it because they get two agents for the price of one.

Does that sound good? Would that work for you?

And while your teammates are setting up searches in MLS, showing homes, and attending inspections, you'll have time to market to get more clients. And of course, check in with your current clients regularly, knowing that your trusted teammates have your back now, and in the future, no matter how many clients you bring in at one time.

Can you picture that? Because there are plenty of agents who have this exact setup and they not only have an abundance of clients, and choices, but they also have balanced lives because they've got teammates, they trust working side by side with them.

So, how do you get to this point? You either need to build a team or join a brokerage that has it waiting for you. Keller Williams is the best brokerage for learning how to build your own team. Relevate is the best brokerage for having a team hired, trained and ready to support you.

However, I suggest that you start by learning about the different kinds of teams. Check out my book,

The Smarter Way to Be a Top Producing Agent, **to figure out what is best for you.**

The kind of team support I've described in this blog can 100% happen for you. You just need to follow the proven path for building your own team, or connecting with a pre-built team, that other agents have followed before you.

Be encouraged. By working hard at working smart, you can achieve all your career and life goals.

Three Horrible Business-Destroying Mistakes

"Before joining Relevate I had been with five different firms over seven years. I owned the last one, which was gratifying to my ego, but was really just another distraction and did nothing to increase my production and take-home earnings.

So I was averaging 17 transactions a year, and that's okay, if by "okay" you mean being stuck way below what I knew I was capable of.

So that's where I was. I definitely had a lot of energy and effort to give my clients. I had real estate skills, but no systems and no support, and no clue how to put that in place for myself.

So I heard about Relevate, and went and drank some beer with the founder, Mike Regan, who it turned out was a legit, published process improvement expert. They had already spent years developing systems and hiring and training licensed agents to handle ALL the basics of marketing and client service, so I could just show up and focus on building my business and not getting wrapped up in all the details.

So I jumped on board, and in the first year I tripled my business from 17 to 52 transactions, and took home incredibly more income to my family than ever before, and also gave my clients much better service. I found out that it's fun to close multiple transactions a week, it's stupid fun.

Anyone can triple their business by leveraging this system. You have to trust it and put in the work. Listen, if you want to talk to a real person about how it works and make sure this isn't fake or smoke and mirrors, just call or text me and I'll be glad to take the time to talk with you about it."

Jed Gronewald

Scan QR code for video

CHAPTER 10

The Truth About Personal Branding: Does It Help Or Hurt?

Scan QR code for video

Is personal branding going to help or hurt your business? You only have so much time, energy, and money to invest in your real estate business, and you want to make the smartest possible decisions to achieve your big goals. There is no shortage of advice about what you need to do to be successful, and if you are not careful, you could spend a lot of time and money doing things that are not helpful and that could actually knock your business sideways. Common "wisdom" includes examples such as:

- You need to build a team

- You need your own separate website that is search-engine-optimized

- You need to spend 10% of your revenue on marketing

So, do you need to build a personal brand to achieve your big real estate sales goals? The answer to that question is yes, for sure! The key question is, how do you do that? Certainly, your name and photo are super important. But should your personal branding efforts also include other elements such as a logo, a unique color scheme, a tagline, and maybe even a name for your business in addition to your personal name? Are these elements necessary, or could they potentially be counter-productive for your business?

We will look at the top real estate agents in the United States and see how they built their personal brands. We will also check out some of our most famous celebrities, all unquestionably brilliant at promoting their personal brands, and see how they are doing it. Finally, we will look at the branding advice being pushed on real estate agents, who is pushing that advice, and what we recommend as the most effective way for agents to promote themselves.

How do the Top Realtors Promote their Personal Brands?

I did a quick Google search to identify the very top real estate agents in the United States (by volume of homes sold) and then I looked at all their social media to see how they represented their personal brands.

The #1 ranked realtor is Alexa Lambert who closed $761M in volume in 2022. Wow, that is a lot of volume. My quick back-of-the-envelope calculation is that she took home about $6 million to her personal bank account last year. She has done a good job promoting herself and her services. Alexa's website includes just her photo, name, and the name of her brokerage. No logos, no color schemes, no taglines, no business name separate from her personal name. Her Instagram & LinkedIn are the same: just her photo and name.

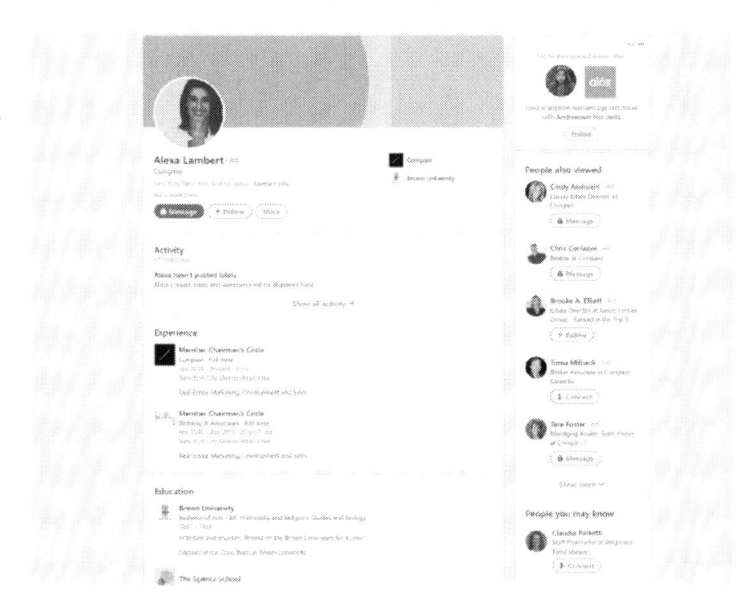

The #2 ranked realtor is Cathy Franklin. She closed $509M in volume in 2022. Her website includes her name, photo, and the name of her brokerage. No logo, color scheme, tagline, or business name different from her personal name. Cathy's Instagram & Facebook include her photo, name, and personal touch with her husband in the photo. Her LinkedIn has just her photo and name.

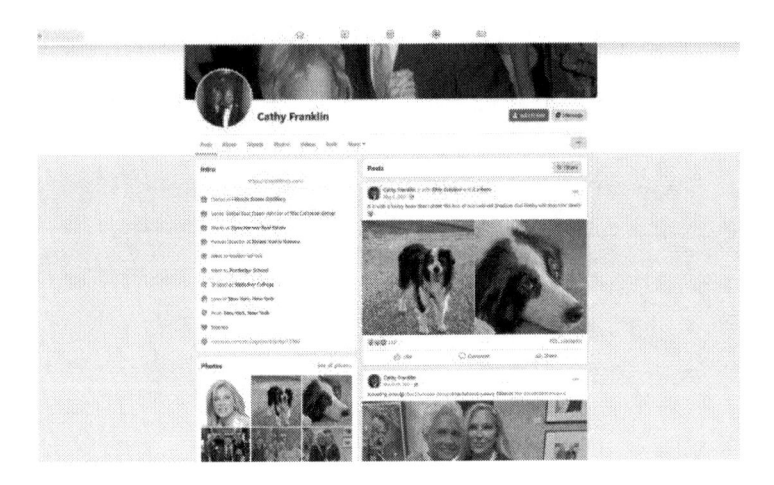

The #3 ranked realtor is Jade Mills with $369M in volume. Jade's website includes her name with the word "Estates" after it. This is a little bit of branding beyond her name and photo. Her Instagram and Facebook are the same while her LinkedIn includes just her name and photo.

The Truth About Personal Branding

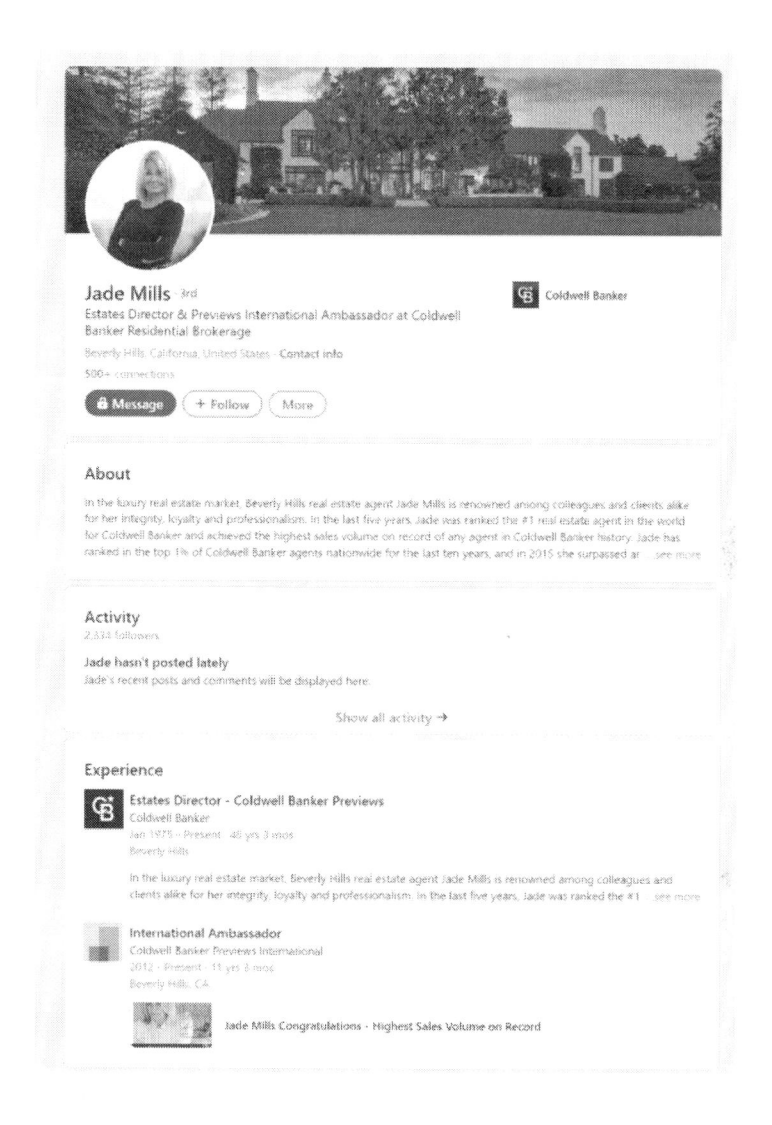

The #4 ranked realtor is Serena Boardman with $365M in volume. Serena's website and Instagram include her name, her photo, and the name of her brokerage. Serena does not appear to have a Facebook or LinkedIn account.

The #5 ranked realtor is Neill Bassi with $286M in volume. Neill's website includes his name and the name of his brokerage. His Instagram includes his name, and he does not appear to have a LinkedIn or Facebook account.

Disclaimer: Okay, I must admit, he was actually #6 and I moved him up because all of the top five agents were women, and just to make the guys feel okay about themselves we needed to have ONE guy. Right? Can you give me this one? **You're killing it, ladies!**

Analysis of the Top US Real Estate Agents' Personal Branding Strategies

So, four of the top five (okay, top six) most successful real estate agents in the United States included only their personal names and photos in their marketing. Only one top agent included anything in addition to their name and photo, and that consisted only of adding the word "Estates" after her name. Based on the success of the other four, you can question if that made any difference for her. From this evidence, it seems that adding a logo, color scheme, tagline, or business name other than your personal name, is **not helpful in growing a real estate business.** But maybe these people are "old fashioned"? How do the top celebrities today promote their personal brands?

Top Celebrity Personal Brands

Let's start with Kim Kardashian. Is there anyone better at promoting herself than Kim? Kim does not appear to have a website for herself but only has websites for her beauty brands. Kim's Instagram advertises two brands representing her products but there are no logos, color schemes, or taglines representing herself. Kim's YouTube channel includes just her name and photo. Kim's Twitter advertises her show (which is her name) and includes her photo. Finally, Kim's video… yep, that video. No doubt it helped her become famous. I did not check it myself, but I am guessing it does not include any logo, taglines, or color schemes.

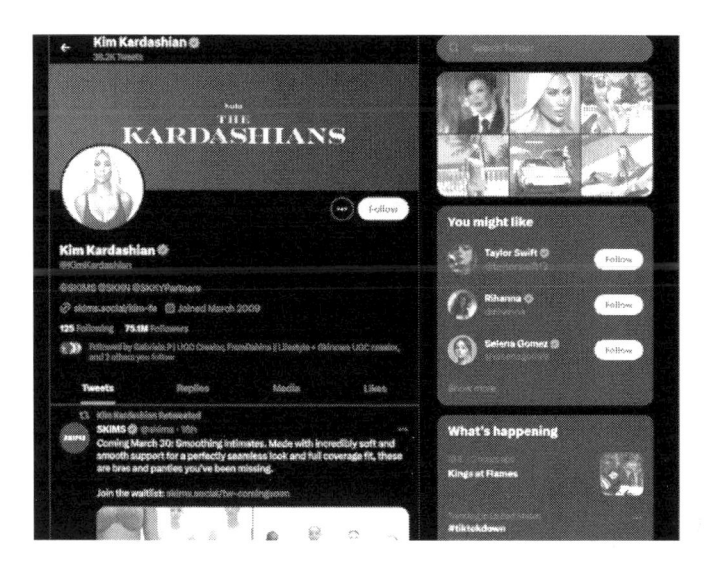

Okay, how about Bruno Mars? In my opinion, Bruno Mars rocks. His original name was Peter Gene Hernandez. He changed his name to Bruno Mars. That is cool, right? His website shows his name and promotes his latest album. Bruno's Instagram has his name and photo with no logo, color scheme, or tagline. Bruno's YouTube channel again, his name, his photo, and promotion of his latest product. No logo, color scheme, or tagline. Bruno's Twitter includes just his name and photo.

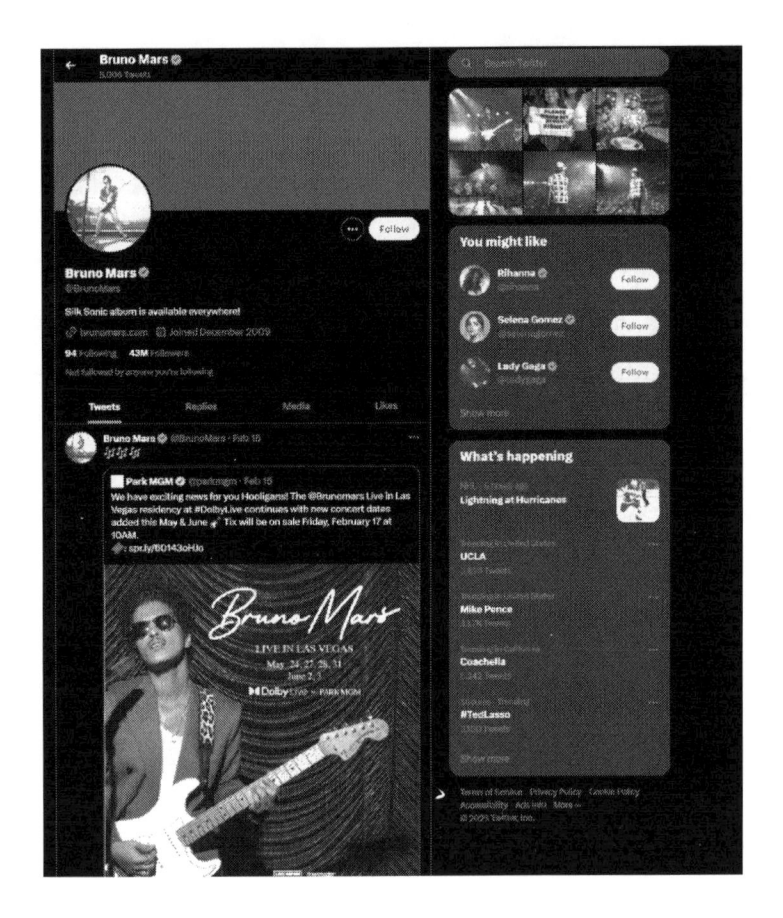

Lastly, let's talk about Jesse Palmer, he is everywhere. He has done a great job building his brand. He is currently an ESPN commentator, the host of The Bachelorette/Bachelor, and a frequent (okay daily) host on the Food Network. How does Jesse promote his brand? He does not have a website dedicated to himself, but his Instagram includes just his name, his photo, and promotion of his projects. On Jesse's YouTube channel, he includes just his name and photo. No logo or color scheme. "Life & Adventure" seems to be a subtitle for his video channel, not a tagline. Finally, Jesse's Twitter with just his name and his photos.

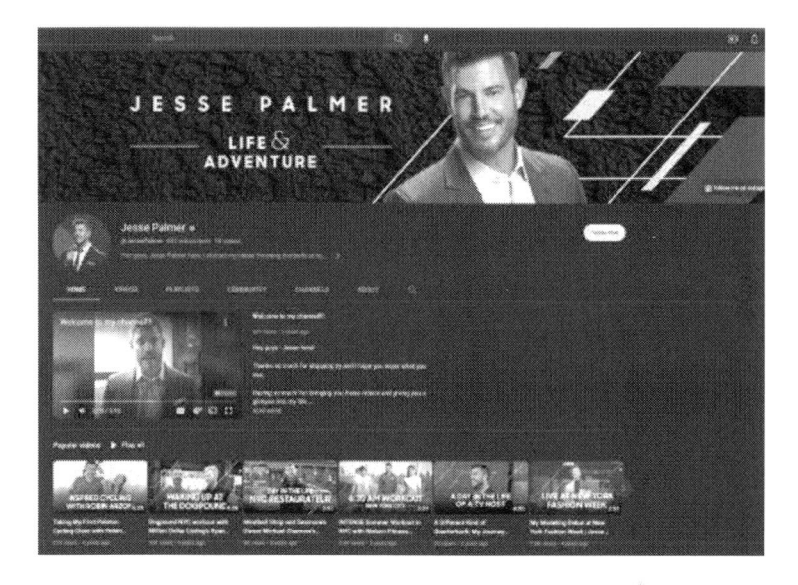

"Your clients are buying you. You are selling yourself as a service, not a service or product separate from yourself."

Analysis of How Top Celebrities Promote Their Personal Brands

Top celebrities are all about personal branding. No doubt they are paying for, and getting, the best possible advice to build their fame. When it comes to promoting themselves, there are no logos, color schemes, taglines, or business names separate from their personal names. The only images they use are their names and photos.

As a Real Estate Agent, Your Name and Your Photo are All the Branding you Need

Your clients are buying you. You are selling yourself as a service, not a service or product separate from yourself. Even if you have a team helping you, they represent you. Therefore, you are your brand, and based on how the best in your business do it, **your name and photo are all the images you need to promote yourself** to the very highest level in the real estate business. Or in any profession for that matter, as we have seen.

But… does it actually hurt to add a logo, color scheme, tagline, and/or a separate business name to your personal name and photo in your marketing? In my opinion, it does. Here is why:

The top agents use their personal name, their photo, and the name of their brokerage in all their marketing. That is what consumers associate with top agents. If you add other visual elements, I think...

At best, it confuses the client because they wonder what those other elements mean. Especially since you are legally required to include your brokerage and their logo in all your marketing. Clients wonder "how many different companies are involved here?". As they say in marketing, if you confuse, you lose.

At worst, it could make you look amateurish. It is expensive and time-consuming to come up with a logo that does not look amateurish. If there is no evidence that logos, color schemes, or taglines help, why take the risk, especially if it will cost you tons of time and money? That is not good business thinking.

Who is Pushing Branding for Real Estate Agents and Why?

Since there is no evidence that logos, color schemes, taglines, and different business names help agents build their business, why are so many agents hot about doing it? This trend started with a few agents being influenced by companies that make money from providing branding services. This includes marketing companies and independent graphic designers telling them they must have a logo, color scheme, and tagline, to compete.

In addition, other companies who market to real estate agents like coaching companies, warranty firms, and business card printers start reprinting "helpful" articles about hot topics on their websites to attract visitors, and soon all of Google is telling agents they must have logos and color schemes. More agents jumped on the bandwagon.

None of the foregoing has any relation whatsoever to what will really help agents grow their businesses.

Let us test this out. I searched Google with the phrase "Will a logo branding help my real estate business?". Of the first twenty results, seven of them were marketing firms offering to design my logo. Nine of them were vendors who wanted to print my logo on a card, t-shirt, or sign and four of them were vendors printing blogs that might attract my attention to their website. None of them actually tried to give me any fact-based business advice about whether I should *have a logo or not* (which was my original question). They all wanted to sell to me, not help me make a smart decision.

Here is the advice I saw about the need for a logo from a home warranty company:

> Your logo is an important part of your overall real estate brand. The logo is often the first thing a potential client will see, so yours should be unique, professional, and relevant. Designing the perfect real estate logo can take time but it is possible to create a memorable logo on your own.
>
> 2-10 Home Warranty
> https://www.2-10.com › blog › 5-considerations-when-d...
> 5 Considerations When Designing Your Real Estate Logo

What on earth does a warranty company know about branding for a real estate agent? This is the result of an intern reposting a paraphrased version of an article he found on a marketing website hoping to get your attention. Here is this warranty company's logo:

Inspiring, right?

Google is not a great place to find business wisdom. For that, you have got to learn from people who have achieved what you want to achieve. We started this article off by showing you what those people do with **no** logos!

If you have already spent time and money on a logo or other additional branding and you are now convinced it will hurt more than help your business, then give yourself permission to learn and streamline your marketing. The most successful businesspeople change directions and simplify quickly once they learn something that makes more sense for their business.

Do I Need My Own Brand to Be a Successful Real Estate Agent?

Yes, but all you need is your own name and a great photo of the beautiful face God gave you.

You may be curious about other ways to grow your real estate business, and/or how to create more take-home income or time for yourself. One question we mentioned earlier was "Does it make sense to build a team (or to continue to manage the one I already have), or is there some other way to get the support I need?"

Alternatively, you may be researching different brokerages to decide which one might be most helpful for you to achieve your business goals. You can find insight into these questions and more by clicking on Become a Relevate Agent on our website relevate.life. Our Relevate for Real Estate Agents YouTube Channel offers valuable content to support you as you advance in your real estate career.

"Obviously everyone in real estate knows the market has slowed quite a bit this year. I will say though, I'm actually having a very good year, and I think a big part of that is the Relevate marketing system.

I know a lot of agents, for their marketing, they purchase leads, or do cold calling or random email blasts or open houses, but I think the reason the Relevate referral-based system is working so well for me in this slower year is that when things are uncertain for people, that's when they really need someone they trust, someone they have a relationship with.

It's just a lot more sustainable even in tough times because people are more, not suspicious of the market, but sort of discerning and more careful.

I'm going to be honest, our marketing team does 70% of the work for me by planning, executing, and delivering the marketing campaigns each month, which gives me a solid and comfortable reason to call and really connect with people. Also, our point system has been key for me, it gamifies the process and definitely keep me motivated and focused to stay consistent with my calls and outreach. As a result, I get a constant stream of referred leads, and I close about one out of every two, so that's strong.

So I'm really grateful. And if I find something good I'm not going to just keep it to myself. I want good for other people. So if you want to meet up I'd be happy to share my story and answer any questions you have. Just text or call me and we can get together."

Matt Minor

Scan QR code for video

Bonus chapters from

THE SMARTER TOP-PRODUCING REAL ESTATE AGENT

How to Maximize Take-Home Income AND Have Amazing Life Balance

MIKE REGAN

REAL ESTATE RE-ENGINEERED BY AN OPERATIONS RESEARCH EXPERT

CHAPTER 1

A Better Way to Be a Top Producing Agent

Scan QR code for video

When you own most normal types of businesses, after you get through the first year or two of working super hard to figure it out and get your customer base established... it gets a lot easier. After that, you don't need to work nearly as much, you have an automatic marketing system working for you, the money keeps coming in (and maybe even increases), and you can take real vacations, during which you don't even have to think about work.

But... it doesn't seem to work that way for real estate agents. You work SO hard (like I did when I got into real estate) to get to $8M, $10M, and $12M in volume, and the process of being a real estate agent doesn't get much more efficient. It just keeps requiring more of your time. At some point, you're thinking, "I like the money, I like real estate, but this just isn't sustainable."

The traditional answer is to build a team. But first, most real estate agents would rather stick a fork in their eye than be a manager and be required to hire, train, and supervise people. And even if you love managing people, the most popular book about building a real estate team, Gary Keller's *The Millionaire Real Estate Agent*, says you only get to keep 62%, 50%, or 39% of your commission (the percentage goes down as your volume goes up). And that's only IF you do it perfectly, so… that doesn't sound like that great of a profit margin, especially considering all the managing you need to do to keep it going.

So, can real estate be like a normal business, where after you work hard, in the beginning, to get it going, you can work fewer hours, and make the same (or more?) money, and take real vacations where you don't have to worry about work the whole time? Yes.

As the author of this book, I'm also the CEO of Relevate Real Estate, and I'll say upfront that one of the approaches to being a successful real estate agent that I'll be talking about throughout is the way we work here at Relevate. However, my only goal is to help you figure out what's best for you, so I'll try to be very unbiased as I explain everything, and I hope you'll feel like I did a good job of that here.

Previously I pointed out that with most businesses, once you work hard to get them going, they get more efficient, and the money keeps coming in and you get the freedom to spend a lot less time working. I experienced this twice with two different businesses, before I got into real estate, first running a manufacturing operation, and then again, after that, with an operations research consulting firm I owned. Maybe that spoiled me because I was expecting the same thing when I got into real estate.

I only got into real estate because I got bored with consulting. For the consulting firm, I had written two books and developed an efficient process to acquire clients and deliver our value.

Process improvement was the kind of consulting we did for our clients, so of course we did it for ourselves too. Our system was successful, I made great money, and I worked about 20 hours a week, but it was the same thing repeatedly… and I was ready for something different. So, I sold the consulting firm and the rights to the books I had written and jumped into real estate.

However, after I was in real estate for about 18 months, closing about 35 transactions annually, I found out the real estate agent business needed some operations research consulting in a big way. I was just way too busy to have an actual life. I said to myself, "This is not cool. There must be a better way, just like when I ran those other businesses, where I could make this process more efficient, and make the same or more money, but NOT have to work so hard, and be able to hang out with my family, AND have real vacations."

So, I applied my consulting experience to the real estate agent business, and made a lot of changes, for my benefit, to the way I did business. And thank goodness, I did find a better way to do it. My life got much better as I grew my business, without having to manage a team, to over $20 million in volume, and my working hours decreased to less than 20 hours per week. In this book I'm going to share the results of that improvement effort with you. So today, I'm not the CEO of Relevate, and instead, I'm going to put my consulting hat on…

Oh wait, that one's from last weekend, I don't know where my consulting hat is. But whatever, the point is I'm going to walk you through the exact analysis I did, as an operations research consultant, on my own real estate business.

I started by analyzing the two traditional normal ways of doing real estate, which are (1) Doing It All Yourself, and (2) Building A Team.

Doing It all Yourself

The advantages of this approach are:
1. Everything's totally in your control, so you know things will be done right because you are the one doing them.
2. You keep almost all the money because you aren't paying anyone.

The disadvantages of this approach all stem from the fact that you must do everything yourself:
1. Either you're too busy serving clients to do any marketing, or you're doing nothing BUT marketing to get more clients because all your current clients closed and there isn't anyone in the pipeline. And that roller coaster gets old quickly.

2. There's no leverage, meaning there isn't any opportunity for you to profit by delegating activities that can be done for a lower hourly rate (like delivering checks, stuffing envelopes, and even some showings) to enable you do to more of the activities that bring in clients and make you lots of money (like calling warm prospects, or stopping by to visit a recently closed buyer),

3. You can't grow your business much beyond about $9 million in volume or 30 transactions (if you're really efficient) so your take-home ("taxable") income can't grow beyond $175-250,000. If you're super-efficient or work a ridiculous number of hours, you might squeeze out more than that, but the bottom line is, that there's definitely a limit.

What all this adds up to, for most agents, is that they sacrifice their life balance, theoretically temporarily, to work very hard to establish a very nice income level, but then when they get there, they find they have to keep working just as hard, just to maintain it. And THAT is not sustainable. And if that's where you are, I get it. I was there too. So, I read Gary Keller's book, *The Millionaire Real Estate Agent*, to learn how to build a team to fix my business and my life.

Building Your Own Team

The advantage of a building a team is supposed to be leverage. This would mean:
1. Being able to delegate lower-hourly-rate tasks so you can focus on the revenue-generating tasks that bring in clients
2. Unlimited volume and income growth, and
3. A better life balance.

The disadvantages of building your own team are:
1. *Building a team requires doing management.* And that, in turn has several disadvantages:
   - Management means hiring, training, and supervising. That sounds awful to most agents.
   - Even if you like management, it takes a lot of time. For many agents who start a team, the amount of time they spend managing is equal to or greater than the amount of time they

save by delegating. So their life-balance gets worse, not better.

- You get paid ZERO when you do management, because it doesn't bring in any business or revenue.

2. As I mentioned earlier, *the profit margin of a team is pretty low*. Gary Keller's book says 62%, at $10M in volume, 50% for $17M, and 39% at $26M, if you do everything perfectly. But almost no one does, so the actual profit percentages are much lower. From the data we've collected, the averages or closer to 50% for $10M, 38% for $17M, and 21% for $26M (the best we've ever seen at $26M is 32.5%).

Now, you may hear some team owners claim to be taking home a higher percentage of total commission, but that is only if they take care of a lot of clients themselves, which means they are giving up a lot of their time, which defeats the purpose of having the team. Then they've got the disadvantages of both doing it on their own and having a team.

As a result, for most agents, when they start a team, their working hours increase and their take-home income decreases, and they usually end the building a team experiment quickly and go back to doing business pretty much by themselves. Which might cause you to ask the question…

So, Why Would Any Agent Have Their Own Team?

Well, when we ask that question, we assume everyone wants maximum take-home income and maximum time to spend with family and on their personal interests. If that is what they want, then sure, having a team doesn't make much sense. However, some agents have different priorities, and we certainly respect that. For example, some agents…

- … like doing management and leading and mentoring others, and they're willing to give up a good amount of take-home income and life balance in order to enjoy that opportunity.

- … don't want to sell. So, they spend money to bring in leads, either by advertising or purchasing from Zillow or realtor.com, and they coach buyers' agents to convert those leads into clients and closings. This is an extremely difficult way to make a living, because not only are they giving up half the commission to buyers' agents, but they're also paying an average of 40% of the commission for the leads in the first place. And for those of you who are into MATH, that only leaves 10% for the owner of the team. It's a tough way to do real estate.

- ... believe the theory in Gary Keller's book that if they just keep at it, they'll build a team they can walk away from, and that will give them continuing passive income while they do other things with their lives. This would have to be a situation where the clients come from some other source than from the agent who owns the team, since that agent is leaving. Mark Spain Real Estate, and all his highway signs about guaranteed offers, is an example of this.

- ... enjoy the admiration of other agents who feel having a team is the ultimate sign of real estate agent success, even if it costs them significant income and life balance. I don't really get this one, but it's a real thing.

So...

Is There a Way for Real Estate Agents to Maximize Take-Home Income AND Have Maximum Life Balance?

That's the question I needed to answer for myself toward the end of my second year in real estate. I was experiencing all the challenges of doing everything myself, and from what I had learned about the Keller Williams team model, I wanted no part of it.

The answer is YES, there is a better way. THANK GOD. Because I wouldn't have stayed in real estate otherwise. NO WAY. Here is what made sense to my operations research process improvement brain:

First, my main issue back then was being so busy and so tired I couldn't even think, and me hiring, training, and supervising people to help me was definitely not the answer. I had some money saved from my time as a successful consultant, so I hired a really good manager, and made her the COO (Chief Operating Officer) for my business, and tasked her with hiring fully licensed agents and a marketing expert, training them to be my support team.

I know what you're doing now, you're saying, "Mike, that's crazy, and you must have been a horrible consultant because obviously hiring a COO dedicated to managing your team would cost way too much". Here is what I say to that… yes, I totally agree. That's why the next step of my plan was to **find other agents who had the same problem as me**, and get them to share the cost of the COO, and as a benefit of doing that, they'd be able to also share in the use of the support team that our COO hired and trained for us.

Soon, I had ten agents working in partnership with me. Each of us paid one-tenth of the cost of the COO, so that cost became very manageable for each of us.

This is the wonderful Trinity French, our first COO, and we would have been lost without her. She's still with us, but she's now a top producing agent.

This is the equally wonderful Christine Nguyen, who was one of the first agents to join our partnership. She's still with us, and by now she's sold over $500M in real estate. She and her husband, Jimmy, take a LOT of vacations. I love that for her.

And this is the super wonderful Jan Carmody, who was our first support team member. She's now one of our brokers-in-charge and still with us, loved by literally everyone.

So, back to our story, we've gotten agents, all sharing the cost of the COO who hired and trained the support team. Now, sharing the support team members turned out to be a huge win for all of us, in three ways:

1. Since we all utilized them, we were able to hire more support team members, which gave us all more flexibility.

2. If any of us needed multiple support team members at once, for example, to staff a big

marketing event or to show homes to several buyers during one weekend day, we had the support capacity to handle it. And,

3. We each only had to pay for the support hours we actually needed, because when one of us wasn't utilized (and paying) for support, several of the other agents were, so our support team members were always being utilized (and paid) by someone, so that gave our support team members job security and enabled us to retain them for the long-term.

So, that's the basic idea. Pretty simple, right?

A key point of working with the licensed support team members is that we'd assign only one of them to be the primary support person for each client, and we introduced them to the client at the very first meeting with that client as a big advantage to them. That was very true because we emphasized that we're not handing the client off in any way, rather the support team member's role was to help us to help them, like a doctor and a nurse taking care of a patient, two for the price of one. The clients loved it.

What happened next is, all of us started selling a lot more houses. And that's because we had a shared marketing plan organized for us, with our input, and campaigns got sent out every month consistently. In addition, we all had more time and energy to keep up with our past clients and our spheres of influence and ask for referrals... because we weren't doing all the client service ourselves anymore.

In addition to that, we all got the flexibility to spend more time with family and actually have... **real vacations** where you could actually turn your phone off... because our clients back home... were covered.

In the end, even though we each did have the added expense of sharing the cost of the COO and paying for however many support team hours we used, we all increased our take-home income a lot, to an average of over 65% of total commission revenue, because all the additional clients and closings way more than made up for the expenses. AND more importantly, we got all that time back for our families and our personal lives.

Since then we've grown a lot and made other process improvements. We expanded our marketing team to plan, produce and implement marketing campaigns or events every month that agents can participate in without having to plan or think about marketing themselves.

We also invested $700,000 (so far) into an amazing software system to track all the client relationships and marketing, and it includes detailed checklists for the support team members to follow so that everything is done right and consistently every time:

Of course, we've hired and trained a lot more client service support team members and they're just amazing people. Finally, we added a listing analysis and preparation team, and of course, a lot more agents have joined our partnership.

"Real estate should (and can be) just like any other business, where you can have plenty of time off and increasing income after the first few hard-working years to get it going."

You CAN Be Very Successful In Real Estate and Have Amazing Life Balance

Real estate should (and can be) just like any other business, where you can have plenty of time off and increasing income after the first few hard-working years to get it going. You just need to have an efficient system, and the traditional advice of "building your own team" is not it.

I hope how I've explained all this makes sense, and if you're at all intrigued then I'm sure you have lot more questions, and I'm guessing the first one is, "What exactly does it cost to do business using the Relevate Business System? So, we've answered that in a very straightforward way. *

*Scan QR code for video

"Before joining Relevate, I was already making a LOT of money, but I was also working a LOT of hours (70/week no exaggeration). I realized "this is exhausting and I need to find another way of doing this business."

I think a BIG misconception in our industry is that in order to grow, you have to build a team. I did do that, I built a team of five people, they were getting half or more of the business, and because of the management responsibilities I was working more than ever. So I went from tired and busy, but just worried about me, to even more tired and busy and also less money in the bank!

Building a team wasn't the solution. I was looking for EASE of managing my business, having it be EASY and NOT difficult, NOT time consuming, and NOT expensive. I did meet an agent who was running her business in a different way, and over coffee she went through what she was doing differently, and I just remember feeling like it was a breath of fresh air, because it did allow me to see another way of being in the business that I love.

I thought it was an amazing solution.

The transition was easier than I could have imagined. My business grew from 12 million to 29.4 million, my take-home income increased dramatically, and because of all the marketing and client service support, I now actually have a life. I'm weightlifting. I'm having ladies night. I'm playing golf.

Then I have this lovely seven year old daughter, and I'm seeing her for long periods of time every single day. And all of my client relationships are very deep.

I want everyone to hear there are other options for how to run your real estate business. I want to talk with you about it. I'd love for you to reach out to me, text or call me and set up a time. It can be really easy and fun. So please, let's try to connect soon. I'd love that."

Adrienne Zetterquist

See QR Code for video

CHAPTER 2

The TRUTH About Building Your Own Real Estate Team

Scan QR code for video

Are you a super busy and successful real estate agent? Have you found that doing it all yourself has gotten stressful and has got your life out of balance? Do you need to build a team to help, or are there alternatives that might actually work better for you?

You may have been told that building a team is the next step. Maybe you've even taken that next step and hired a few people. But is hiring, training, and managing other people really what you want to do? Are there alternative ways to get the support you need? Yes, but each alternative has advantages and disadvantages.

Talking about the hard stuff is never easy, and that is why most brokerages shy away from this type of content.

I've been where you are. At the beginning of my career as a real estate agent, I grew my own business quickly from zero to eighty-eight transactions per year. I cannot give myself all the credit though. I started with a part-time team and then I built an industry-standard "MREA" team (as described in Gary Keller's book, *The Millionaire Real Estate Agent*). Finally, I connected into the already-built and fully-trained Relevate support team.

In this chapter, we will walk through these **three alternative ways** of getting the support team you need to continue growing at the rate your talent deserves. We will break down the "pros" and "cons" of each type of team and suggest what type of agent-team duo will work best. You will be one step closer to having the right support team for you.

What are the Different Types of Real Estate Teams

The Part-Time Team

This first alternative is a low-risk, "toe in the water" approach consisting of using part-time help such as

- An unlicensed assistant (often a family member) to stuff and stamp envelopes for marketing.

- Using apps such as Showami or "partnership deals" with other agents in your brokerage to get help showing homes or attending inspections when you are busy.

- A part-time transaction coordinator (usually unlicensed), either hired by you or offered by your brokerage.

Normally, to save money and maintain control, an agent with a part-time team does all they can themselves and only delegates the overflow to others.

The Pros Include:

- Low risk with low and instantly controllable expenses.

- Enables an agent to increase transaction volume by about 20% and take some limited time off.

- The agent keeps a high percentage of the gross commission income.

The Cons Include:

- Customer service handled by team members is not at the highest level due to a lack of processes and thorough training.

- Potential income level is limited by the capacity of this type of team to handle much growth.

- Most agents will feel that the management responsibility necessary even for a small, part-time team is distracting and not enjoyable.

The part-time team is best for agents who want to do things their way and also want to avoid the risk and responsibility of hiring full-time people.

The Industry Standard "Millionaire Real Estate Agent" (MREA) Team

The second alternative to get the support you need is to build an MREA team. This model became the "industry standard" when Gary Keller interviewed hundreds of high-volume agents in many brokerages across the US. He documented, in *The Millionaire Real Estate Agent* book, how they had structured their teams and the standard process they used to build those teams from scratch. As a result of this book, Keller Williams became "the place to build a team" and that was a big part of how Keller Williams Realty grew so fast.

Here is the implementation process for this type of team:

- Hire an assistant to do administrative tasks.

- Hire your first buyers' agent to take care of your buyer clients since buyers normally take much more time than sellers.

- Invest in more lead sources, like advertising and purchased leads (Zillow, Realtor.com, Homelight, etc.) and hire more buyer's agents to convert the buyer leads from those sources and work them (you keep the seller leads).

- Hire a "listing coordinator" who is like a buyer's agent for sellers, converting and serving seller leads.

- Leave the team to do everything without you. The leads keep coming in and they keep converting them while you get the profits.

The Pros Include:

- Truly unlimited transaction and volume growth potential.

- The best choice for having a big team and a well-known personal brand.

- Great opportunity to lead and grow other people.

- The team leader has complete control over all marketing, processes, and systems.

- Leaders of these types of teams often leave their current firm to establish themselves as independent brokerages.

The Cons Include:

- By far the most costly type of team, due to the need to pay 50%+ of the commission to buyers' agents (mostly to compensate for their effort to convert lower-quality leads) and the high cost of purchasing and/or advertising to get those leads. As a result, team leaders rarely keep more than 35% of the total team gross commission.

- Not all agents enjoy the demanding and constant management responsibility required to lead this type of team.

- High turnover of buyers' agents (whom the team leader trained and mentored, and who are now leaving to compete against them) can be frustrating.

The MREA team is best for agents who want to start and run their own business from scratch, including managing and motivating other people. Being seen as very successful by other agents is also a motivating factor for some team leaders.

The Relevate Team

The third way to have a support team is a "Relevate Team". In this support team model, the brokerage has already hired and fully trained licensed professionals who immediately become your full-service team when you join the brokerage. These team members include:

- **Marketing professionals:** Plan your marketing in advance for the entire year; design, write, produce, address, stuff, stamp, and deliver all marketing materials.

- **Licensed agents:** These "Client Service Managers" partner with you to do all client service work on your behalf such as searching for homes, researching client questions, showing homes, writing contracts (directed by you), arranging and attending inspections, negotiating due diligence agreements, arranging repairs, scheduling and attending closings, and more!

- **The Listing Success Team:** Analyze sellers' homes to identify improvements that will increase their sales price and reduce their "days on market." Consult with sellers and teach them how to prepare their homes for sale, and give them the specifics of colors, styles, and vendors for any improvements. They also manage the improvement project as needed, stage the home, and arrange for professional photography.

"**The Relevate Team is best for agents who want to keep things simple and focus primarily on selling, delivering great client service, and still making very good money.**"

The idea of this model is to free up the agent (referred to as the "Sales Agent" at Relevate) to do what **only they can and want to do**: build relationships with their sphere of influence and past clients to bring in growing numbers of referred and repeat clients.

The Pros Include:

- Unlimited transaction and volume growth potential

- Because of the economies of scale Relevate realizes by providing standardized marketing and client service support to a large number of agents, the cost of the support is reasonable. As a result, Relevate leadership guarantees agents who follow the process correctly will take home at least 65% of gross commission.

- Excellent life balance, ability to spend plenty of time with family and take "real vacations" (not tied to phone or computer)

- Collaborative, non-competitive environment among agents

The Cons Include:

- The Relevate system is standardized and must be followed closely to ensure the high take-home income and life balance results. As a result, the Relevate experience can feel less "entrepreneurial." Consistent with this, Relevate does not support personal branding (other than your name and photo) in your marketing.

- Agents have to get comfortable with the idea of delegating so much of the marketing and client service and trusting everything will be done right.

- This structure can seem "expensive" to individual agents who have never had a support team and are accustomed to keeping 85%+ of their gross commission income (although at a significantly lower amount of total commission).

- Less opportunity for "creative expression" since the firm plans and executes almost all marketing campaigns.

The Relevate Team is best for agents who want to keep things simple and focus primarily on selling, delivering great client service, and still making very good money. This team model is perfect for agents who do not want to have to worry about anything else. We feel this is the best choice for agents who need a better life balance, especially for moms with younger children.

Which Type of Team Is Right for Me?

Successful real estate agents often have more clients than they can handle on their own, and start to experience high levels of stress and out-of-balance lives. They know they need a support team but may not know what kinds of support teams are possible and how they work.

Now that we've walked through the basics for all three types of support teams for real estate agents like you, you may have a lot of questions. Covering the pros and cons of each is really just the beginning. You have a big decision to make, and you might be asking yourself, for example, how does each type of team:

- Ensure my clients will get great quality service?
- Help me build my personal real estate brand?
- Maximize my take-home income?
- Give me more life balance and real vacations?

These comparisons are critical because depending on what is most important for you and your business, one type of team might be perfect for you while another might be completely wrong.

Purchase your copy of <u>*The Smarter Top Producing Real Estate Agent: Maximize your Take-Home Income and Have Amazing Life Balance*</u> *on Amazon, or if you are in the Raleigh, NC area email mike@relevate.life to arrange a time to pick up a complimentary copy at our office.*

"So, I got to 6 million in volume in my first year pretty quickly. But once I got there, I was still very hungry. What I really wanted was to take off exponentially. I wanted to be at 10 million, 15 million, 20 million, relatively quickly.

Most agents, to do that, need to change their business model because they need to hire and train people to support them, or they start giving buyer leads to other people and giving them half the commission. I didn't have to do that though... because at my firm they actually hire and train people to BE my team, to be that support you need to go to the next level. They do most of the marketing and client service FOR me so I can just continue focusing on growing my volume without having to build a team or manage anyone.

I got to 16.5 million in my second year, and this year, even though 2023 was a down year, I closed $15M in 2023 and went into 2024 with an additional $7M already pending!

But... what I'm happiest about is I got to this level, and it didn't wreck my life balance or take away time from my wife and young children. It was just kind of 3a smooth progression because of the support.

Listen, part of who I am is I want to share what's good with other people. I want other agents to have the same experience I'm having, to have the exponential growth I've experienced. If any of what I've said resonates with the questions you're asking, I'm happy to have a conversation. Reach out to me, and we'll set up a time and I'll explain what my life has looked like here and what you could expect here as well."

Pete Marston

See QR Code for video

Bonus chapters from

THE
SMARTER WAY TO
BUY AND SELL YOUR HOME

Inside Information from the
Mad Scientist of Residential
Real Estate

MICHAEL D. REGAN

CHAPTER 1

The 16 Things Your Agent Must Do When Selling Your Home

Part 1

Scan QR code for video

There are 16 crucial things your agent must do for you when selling your home if you want the highest price in the shortest amount of time.

Before I got into real estate, I was a process improvement consultant and the author of two books on the subject. Then, as a top-producing real estate agent, I sold over 750 homes in my 17-year career. Now, as the founder and CEO of Relevate Real Estate, I'm back to spending all my time on process improvement.

In this chapter, I am going to explain the first eight of 16 things your agent MUST do for you when selling your home, and why each of these is crucial for the successful sale of your home. Let's go.

1. Bring a Solid Plan to Get You the **HIGHEST PRICE** in the **SHORTEST AMOUNT OF TIME.**

According to a survey by the National Association of Realtors, when homeowners are ready to sell their home, they want the highest price in the shortest amount of time. And in fact, sellers actually prioritize "fast sale" as slightly more important than "highest price".

That's a little surprising but it's actually understandable. Selling a home is a big project and there are a lot of reasons to want to get it done quickly. For example, so you can buy another home or, maybe you already bought that other home, and you don't want to make two mortgage payments forever. Right?

Most homeowners, and even most real estate agents assume those two important objectives (high price and fast sale) conflict with one another. Like "Which do you want, a high price or a fast sale?"

But... if your agent does it right, as I'll explain, your home will have maximum showing traffic the minute it goes on the market. This will create a sense of urgency, which quickly produces the highest possible offers and maybe even a bidding war. That's what will get you the highest price in the shortest amount of time.

This all starts with how well your agent executes The Four P's of Home Selling:

- Preparation

- Price

- Presentation

- Promotion

Let's dig into these "FOUR P's". PREPARATION and PRICE go together.

To get Preparation and Price right, your agent must first...

2. Give You an Accurate Analysis Of The As-Is Selling Price Of Your Home

But your agent must not stop there. They must also...

3. Give you a Report About Potential Improvements that Will Make You an Additional Profit When You Sell

Unless your home is brand new, there are always opportunities for you to spend a little on the right improvement projects and make thousands of dollars more on the sale of your home.

This report should list:

1. The potential improvements
2. The cost of each

"Unless your home is brand new, there are always opportunities for you to spend a little on the right improvement projects and make thousands of dollars more on the sale of your home."

What Your Agent Must Do To Sell Your Home

3. The new (and higher) sales price of your home, and

4. The PROFIT from those improvements (the increase in sales price minus the cost of making the improvements)

The research to produce this report is a ton of work, as you might imagine, and the best real estate firms have internal teams to help their agents do this analysis quickly and accurately. Also, your agent should never "push" you to make these improvements, because it's your house; but as a basic part of their job, they need to inform you of the opportunity to make more money so you can make an informed decision.

If you do decide to move ahead with the improvement plan, your agent should...

4. Give You a Detailed Report of the Best Styles, Colors and Vendors for the Improvements

For example, if you decide to move forward with your agent's recommendation for new countertops, they should suggest a specific type (granite v quartz), a style/color, a provider from which to get the material, a vendor to install them (and often a backsplash as well), a recommendation for a specific sink and faucet, and a plumber to hook it up. They should provide the same detailed help for flooring, paint, window treatments, etc.

All of what I've explained so far should be provided at no cost to you. It should be part of the normal service, every time, by a reputable agent.

In addition, your agent should be able to arrange for...

5. Expert Project Management in Case You Would Prefer Someone Else To Manage The Improvement Process

Most homeowners prefer not to be involved in managing the improvements. This is a service you'll need to pay for as it requires a lot of additional work. The cost is usually between $500 and $2500, depending on how big your improvement opportunities are.

And by the way, when it comes to project management or recommending vendors and suppliers, your agent should not be making any money from any of that, or getting any kickbacks from vendors. That's not cool. Their advice should be 100% based on what's best for you, not based on other ways for them to make a buck.

Your agent should only make money when they get the job done by selling your home.

Okay, so let's assume, like 80% of homeowners in our experience, you want to move forward with the improvement opportunities your agent presented to you because you're ready for that great short-term return-on-investment.

As a result, there's a period of time when we wait for improvements to be completed. During this time, your agent must be...

6. Marketing Your Home Aggressively Even Before Your Home is "On the Market"

"Mike, what the heck do you mean, 'marketing my home before it's on the market?'" Here's inside scoop: normally agents are not permitted to market your home until it is activated on the MLS.

However, there is a loophole that allows them to market your home to other agents in their firm and to those agents' buyers. Your agent should be doing that aggressively... and actually that should have started well before, because they would have brought a list of buyers who have criteria similar to your home, to that first meeting with you.

Now you might be thinking, "But Mike... I thought we didn't want to expose our home to the market until it was fully prepared?" But what if, before you're too far down the road with the improvements, someone wants to give you an offer that's significantly above your as-is selling price, maybe even close to the post-improvement price? You'd want to know about that, right? You'd probably say "sure, let's get this thing over with and move on!"

Well, that's why marketing is so important. The psychology of buyers is such that when a home is not available to the general public, it's more exciting; there's a feeling of "I can grab this home before anyone else knows about it" and since they know you have an alternative plan in the works to get more for the home as a result of the improvements, they're really bidding against that plan. So, they've got to come with a strong offer if they want you to consider selling early.

If your agent is really on top of this strategy, this can happen for up to 20% of all of their listings. And they need to be doing their best to make that happen for you.

Once your home is fully prepared, and if it isn't already sold pre-market, your agent must deliver on that 3rd "P" and...

7. PRESENT Your Home Perfectly for Maximum Early Showing Volume

I'll explain the details of that in a moment but first, to PRESENT your home for the best results, your agent cannot fail to ...

8. Stage Your Home in the Smartest, Most Cost-Effective Way Possible

Let's talk about staging for a moment. The data shows that when done right, staging is the single best return-on-investment you can do when selling your home. 10 to 1. That means if you invest $750 in staging the right way, you'll increase your selling price by $7,500.

So, what's the right way to stage, and why does it give such a good return?

Based on years of testing, what makes sense in staging is wall hangings like paintings and mirrors, and accessories in the kitchen and master bathroom. Staging with furniture is very expensive, and it does not have an additional impact on the selling price.

Why does staging give such a good ROI? Because staging makes the photography look better, and if buyers don't like the photos in the MLS, they won't schedule a showing. Then, when buyers visit your home, they get to experience those extra touches in person and are reminded what they liked so much in the photos. That's why, by the way, virtual Photoshop staging is counterproductive.

Here's a secret. BUYERS DON'T BUY HOMES. They buy the feeling they have when they're in the home. And good staging is a big part of making that feeling happen. That's why staging gives such a high ROI.

Are there a few sellers that have their home looking so perfect, with the most current decorating style, that they don't need staging? Yes, but that only accounts for 10%. Your agent should be able to give you accurate advice, but don't lose out on a 10 to 1 return just to save a few up front bucks. Staging isn't a cost, it's an investment.

Again, make sure your agent doesn't make money by staging. Otherwise, is their advice truly trustworthy?

The very best real estate firms have internal staging professionals with warehouses full of the latest styles of wall hangings and accessories. Watch out for staging firms that try to save money by not regularly updating their inventory. Out-of-style decorations will reduce, not increase, the selling price of your home.

Okay, so once the staging is completed, it's time for your agent to deliver the rest of the third "P", PRESENTATION. Your agent should be scheduling and PAYING for:

- PROFESSIONAL measurements and great-looking floor plans to upload to the MLS. And...
- PROFESSIONAL photography (with professional equipment and wide-angle lenses). If your agent is doing it with an phone, that's not going to be good for you.

Once everything is done perfectly to present your home, your agent really needs to kick the marketing into high gear.

To read Part 2 of "The 16 Things Your Agent Must Do When Selling Your Home", purchase your copy of <u>The Smarter Way to Buy and Sell a Home</u> on Amazon, or if you are in the Raleigh, NC area email mike@relevate.life to arrange a time to pick up a complimentary copy at our office.

CHAPTER 2

How to Find the BEST Home for the BEST Price

Scan QR code for video

In this chapter, I'll share five smart tips about your financing, whether or not you should use an agent, when you should start your search, what criteria you shouldn't leave out of your search parameters, and finally why you should take a walk before you make an offer.

1. Get Your Financing Figured Out

Before you know what homes to consider, you need to know how much you can afford, and that comes down to the monthly payment amount. Between loan products and new lending rules, variable interest rates and credit score surprises, most buyers are looking in the wrong price range (too high or too low). Ask your real estate broker for a referral to a mortgage lending specialist with at least five years' experience. Based on your preferred monthly payment, income, and credit scores, they will review all your loan and down-payment options and write you a "pre-qualification letter" stating what purchase price you can afford.

The seller's agent will need this letter before they can consider your offer. A "pre-approval letter" (as opposed to a pre-qualification letter) require much more labor on your part to provide additional paperwork and verification, but since listing agents don't care about this at all, it will not help you at all when making an offer on a home, so skip it. The listing agent will either trust the reputation of your agent who is making the offer, OR if they have any real concern, they'll ask permission to talk to your lender, which you should grant.

You will get the best advice and rates from a mortgage broker who specializes in residential loans and has access to a large variety of loan products. Loan officers who work for one of the big banks, such as Wells Fargo and Bank of America, tend to focus exclusively on their own products. Retail bank locations are busy with a wide variety of services such as checking, savings, business and auto loans, and normally offer limited lending options, so they are rarely competitive. One exception is the State Employees Credit Union. If you are a member, you should definitely talk to them about your purchase.

Shop for the best rate for your family but think twice about switching away from a lender who invested their time to give you advice and help, just to save an eighth of a point. Anyone can quote you a lower rate, but that lender may drop the ball later and cost you money or delay your closing. Do not use internet lenders, out-of-state lenders, or any lender who was not referred to you, unless you like surprise rate hikes the day before your closing, when it is too late to react.

A great mortgage broker can sometimes even lower your rate after you lock it in, by moving you to a different lender if the rates go down before closing. The best brokers will call and offer it without you having to ask. You will only find that kind of broker by referral.

Finally, when your mortgage broker asks for additional paperwork, get it to them immediately. They cannot control what the underwriter will ask for or when, and if you are late delivering the paperwork, your closing might be late also.

2. Use a Real Estate Agent

Yeah, okay, I'm a real estate agent and I hang out with a lot of real estate agents. But here's why I'm suggesting that you use a real estate agent when you buy...

As a buyer, the commission for your agent is almost always paid by seller of the home through the firm that lists the home you end up buying. So, depending on how you look at it, either (a) you don't pay any commissions when you use an agent to help you, or (b) the commission you pay is rolled into the price of the home, and therefore into the 30-year loan you got to purchase the home.

In addition, a good real estate agent will help you find the right home in the right area, guide you away from big mistakes, and negotiate a better deal for you. Some buyers think they will save money by not having an agent. Think again. The seller has agreed to pay a certain commission rate to the listing agent, regardless of whether the buyer is represented or not. If you don't have an agent, the listing agent will keep the entire amount, and you will miss out on the benefit of professional advice.

Beware of agents who offer you part of their commission as a "buyer rebate." This may be a sign they are struggling to survive as a real estate agent, or doubt their own value, and as a result may not be competent to represent you.

"A good real estate agent will help you find the right home in the right area, guide you away from big mistakes, and negotiate a better deal for you."

3. Start Early

Most buyers purchase a home that doesn't fully match their original criteria, because their criteria evolves and changes as they look at homes. If you start looking too late, you might buy the wrong home, because you haven't had that time to think. It makes sense to start looking and exploring long before you are ready to buy, to give yourself time to learn and think about what you see. A good agent will be patient and will prioritize your needs and timeline above any other interests. Meet with that good real estate agent and tell them your criteria. Then look at a map and ask them what areas are appreciating in value, and what areas to avoid.

Your broker will start sending you properties by email. Sort through them and pick the ones you like the most. When you have time, drive by these homes and see what you think about the neighborhood and the commute to work. By doing this and taking your time, you'll find neighborhoods you never knew existed. You have to decide what geographic area you want to live in before you decide which specific home you want to purchase. The right house in the wrong area, is the wrong house, right? At this stage you are trying to figure out the right area.

Continue to look for homes on Realtor.com and Zillow as well as on the search page on your broker's web site. You'll end up finding homes you like that do actually meet your original criteria. No problem. That's the whole point. Tell your agent about these, change your criteria if you want to, and they'll send you more homes to consider.

If you see a home in the middle of all this that you absolutely love, call your agent and tell them you want to see it ASAP. No harm in looking, and if it is the perfect home, maybe it makes sense to move a little earlier than you planned.

4. Know Your Criteria

It's common to forget a criteria that ends up being really important to you later. Better to think about it early on and have it on your list. Here is a solid list of criteria for you to consider:

The Smarter Top Producing Real Estate Agent

- Price Range
- Detached/Townhome/Condo
- Number of Bedrooms
- Living Area Square Footage
- Master Bedroom Downstairs
- Number of Bathrooms
- Geographic Area
- School Districts
- Acreage
- Age of Home
- Lot Type (Corner/Cul-De-Sac)
- HOA Dues
- Number of Garage Bays
- Commute Time to Work
- Direction House Faces
- County/City
- Water Supply
- Waste Services
- Fenced Yard
- Exterior (Brick/Vinyl/Etc.)
- Community Pool
- Golf Course Community
- Screened Porch
- Short-Sale/Foreclosure
- "Fixer Upper"
- Deck
- Pool
- Storage Shed
- Private Lot
- Storage Space
- Extra Parking
- Flat Lot
- Basement
- One Story
- Fireplace

Tell your real estate agent everything you want in your next home. If your search results in too many homes to choose from, you can add to your criteria to narrow it down. If not enough homes match your criteria, you can make your criteria less specific.

5. Walk the Neighborhood Before Making an Offer

Before committing to purchasing a home, take a few slow walks through the neighborhood at different times of day. Listen for barking dogs. Look for children playing if that is important to you (because the law prohibits your agent from discussing anything related to "familial status", even whether there are kids in a neighborhood). Introduce yourself to a few neighbors. Tell them which home you are thinking about and ask them what they know. Neighbors love to talk, and you might be glad you listened.

Purchase your copy of The Smarter Way to Buy and Sell a Home on Amazon, or if you are in the Raleigh, NC area email mike@relevate.life to arrange a time to pick up a complimentary copy at our office.

We hope this book has been very valuable for your real estate career. We'd love to hear from you about what you found most helpful, or about any questions you have. Send an email to mike@relevate.life and we promise to respond ASAP!

Made in the USA
Columbia, SC
06 January 2025